THE
WORKING
ADDICT

DAVID CAPLOVITZ

THE
WORKING
ADDICT

M. E. SHARPE, INC., WHITE PLAINS, N.Y.

Library of Congress Catalog Card Number: 77-94070
International Standard Book Number: 0-87332-116-2

Printed in the United States of America

CONTENTS

For Abigail and Gideon,
the joys of my life

THE
WORKING
ADDICT

INTRODUCTION

Until recently, drug addiction was seen as a phenomenon of the streets, far removed from the work place. It was widely assumed that the heroin addict was too unstable to hold a full-time job. But in the past seven years a number of firms have discovered that just as they are not immune to alcoholism, so they are not free of a drug problem. In industry after industry firms have found that some of their employees were using and abusing hard drugs.* To shed light on this overlap of the worlds of drugs and work, we have carried out a survey of addicts who held full-time jobs for an extensive period while they were addicted. This study thus deals with a deviant group within a deviant population — for most addicts do not work full-time, and of course, most full-time workers are not addicts. How these working addicts were able to integrate their work lives with their drug habit, the various ways in which their drug habit impinged upon their job, their relationships with employers and co-workers, the ways in which their work roles influenced their drug habit, and the degree to which they participated in the drug culture, as well as the work culture, are the major themes covered by this study.

---

*For a recent study documenting drug abuse in industry, see Louis Lieberman and David Caplovitz, The Drug Problems of Industry, Graduate School and University Center of the City University of New York, 1976.

The Sample

This survey is based on face-to-face interviews with 555 addicts in treatment who held full-time jobs for at least three months while they were addicted. The sample was drawn from the clientele of a number of drug treatment programs in New York City, both methadone maintenance and drug-free programs. The specific programs represented in this survey and the number of interviews conducted with the clients of each is shown in Appendix 1. (Appendix 2 reproduces the questionnaire used.) The majority of the respondents came from methadone maintenance programs, for the simple reason that most of the addicts in treatment are affiliated with such programs. In all, some 71% of the sample was recruited from methadone maintenance programs, and 29% was found in drug-free treatment programs.*

The Organization of the Study

Chapter 1 describes the kinds of people who make up the sample of working addicts. They are compared with the addict population on a number of social characteristics. We will be able to see if working addicts differ from typical addicts and the ways in which they are similar to and different from the general population. Chapter 2 describes the drug habit of these working addicts, the kinds of drugs they used, the amount of money they spent on drugs, the extent of multiple drug use, and the degree of their dependence on drugs during the working day. The third chapter deals with the work history of these addicts, the kinds of jobs they held, the industries in which they worked, their attitudes toward their jobs, and the amount of money they earned. Chapter 4 examines the interaction between their drug habit and their labor force participation. For example, were addicts who

---

*For the city as a whole, 77% of addicts in treatment were in methadone maintenance programs, and 23% in drug-free programs. Our sample thus overrepresents, slightly, drug-free programs.

became addicted at an early age as likely to get a decent job as addicts who became addicted when older? Did those who earned more spend more money on their habit? Chapter 5 considers the various ways in which the drug habit intruded upon the addict's job, and Chapter 6 deals with the social context of addiction at the work place. Was the employer aware of the addict's habit, and if so, what was his attitude? Did the addict's co-workers know of his habit, and how did they feel about it? Were other co-workers addicted, and was there any traffic in drugs at the work place? In short, Chapter 6 deals with the extent to which a drug culture had intruded upon the work place. Chapter 7 deals with the extent to which these working addicts were involved in the traditional life-style of addiction, criminal behavior and association with fellow addicts. Did they hide their habit from everyone but themselves and identify primarily with the world of work, or did they participate in the two worlds of addiction and work simultaneously? Finally, Chapter 8, the concluding chapter, summarizes the main findings of the research and discusses their implications for social policy.

Acknowledgements

Large scale empirical research requires a team of researchers for its successful execution. This study is no exception. I am particularly grateful to my colleague Dr. Louis Lieberman, who assisted me in developing the questionnaire and took major responsibility for contacting the drug treatment programs and obtaining their cooperation. Dr. Lieberman assumed primary responsibility for the sampling and recruiting, training, and supervising the interviewers. Audrey Blumberg, Nancy Adams, and Judy Morris not only served as interviewers, but they also were in charge of coding the data, preparing the code book, and writing memoranda on special subgroups of addicts such as those who earned a great deal of money and those who used a number of drugs. I am also grateful to these women for contributing to the high morale of the research team. Louis Genevie assumed primary responsibility for the computer tabulations, and he generated most of the tables for this study. I am happy to acknowledge his invaluable help. The project secretary, Darienne Granville, helped in innumerable ways, including the typing of the final report. I am most grateful to Darienne for calling my attention to a host of errors that crept into the manuscript. Finally, I wish to thank my friend, Virginia White, the Director of Sponsored Research and Program Funding at the Graduate School of the City University of New York, for her help when I was writing the original proposal and for her encouragement throughout the project.

This research was carried out under Grant Number DA00800-01, 02 of the National Institute on Drug Abuse, and I am particularly grateful to Ms. Eleanor Carroll of NIDA for her interest and support for this research.

1

Social Characteristics of Working Addicts

Are working addicts representative of the addict population, or does the fact that they held jobs when most addicts do not make them more like the general population of nonaddicts? This chapter deals with this question. We shall compare the working addicts with two other groups: the addict population in New York City and the general population of adults of comparable age to addicts.

Information on addicts in New York City was obtained from the research office of the state's addiction agency (Office of Drug Abuse Services). The files of this agency covered 33,279 addicts in treatment, 71% of whom were located in methadone maintenance programs, and 29% in drug-free treatment programs. Data on the general population were taken from the 1970 census. To make the comparisons more meaningful, we have limited the census data to residents of Manhattan, Brooklyn, and the Bronx, the three boroughs from which the working addicts were sampled.

It is important to keep in mind that although this study deals with addicts who held jobs, our sample is by no means representative of this group. Rather, we are dealing with a subset of working addicts: those who for one reason or another ended up in treatment programs. A fourth significant group is thus missing from this chapter: working addicts who did not enter treatment programs, the so-called "hidden addicts." These hidden addicts are more successful as addicts than those who enter treatment programs, for they have been able to make it on their own. There can be no disputing that such a group, however

7

large, does exist. Most of the working addicts in our sample
were members of this group for many years before they somehow failed and found their way to a treatment program. Although
virtually nothing is known about these "hidden addicts," it will
be possible to make some inferences about this missing group
from the data on hand.

Drug addiction is primarily an affliction of the young. It has
been said that if a person can get past the age of 25 without being
addicted to drugs, he will be immune to this scourge. And many
addicts apparently are able to grow out of their dependency on
drugs as they approach middle age. It comes as no surprise
then that the working addicts were concentrated in the 20- to
29-year-old group. But the critical question is whether they
were younger or older than addicts in general and how different
their age structure is from the general population. The answers
to these questions appear in Table 1.1. (The age categories for
the addict population in treatment differ by one year from the
age categories in the other two groups, and in this one table
people 50 and over are included in the data on the general population.)

Table 1.1

Ages of General Population, Working Addicts,
and All Addicts (in %)

Age	General population	Working addicts	All addicts	
17-24	18	39	25 and under	55
25-29	10	36	25-30	20
30-34	8	14	31-35	11
35-39	8	4	36-40	7
40 and over	56	6	41 and over	7

That addiction is a problem of the young is immediately evident when the ages of addicts, whether they work, are compared
with the ages of the general population. Only small fractions of

the addict groups are 40 years of age or older, whereas fully
56% of the general population 17 years of age and older are 40
or more. Substantial majorities of both working addicts and all
addicts are under 30, compared with only 28% of the general
population. The age differences between working addicts and
all addicts shown by columns two and three are also of significance. Addicts in general tend to be much younger than working
addicts. Thus 55% of all addicts in treatment are 25 or younger,
compared with 39% of the working addicts. This is not surprising, for some people become addicted at very early ages, before
they are old enough to hold a job. Thus among all addicts there
are a number who are under 17, whereas none of the working
addicts were younger than 17. With respect to age, then, working addicts depart from addicts in general and are more like
the general population.

   Just as addiction is a youth phenomenon, so it tends to be male
dominated as well, as can be seen from Table 1.2 which shows
the sex distribution among working addicts, all addicts, and the
general population. (In this and all subsequent tables the general
population is limited to those between the ages of 17 and 49.)

Table 1.2

Sex Distribution in General Population,
Working Addicts, and All Addicts (in %)

Sex	General population	Working addicts	All addicts
Male	46	74	77
Female	54	26	23

   In the general population, women outnumber men 54 to 46%,
but in the addict population men clearly dominate. Among all
addicts, 77% are men, and among working addicts, 74%. As in
the age table, working addicts are somewhat closer to the general population than are all addicts.

   How the three samples compare on marital status is shown
in Table 1.3.

Table 1.3

Marital Status of General Population,
Working Addicts, and All Addicts (in %)

Marital status	General population	Working addicts	All addicts
Single	34	43	59
Married	55	38	23
Separated-divorced	9	17	17
Widowed	2	2	1

If marriage is a mark of stability among adults, then clearly
the general population is more stable than the addict population,
as a majority of New Yorkers between 17 and 49 are married,
whereas only a minority of the addicts are married. But again
the working addicts fall in the middle between all addicts and
the general population. Thus they are more likely to be married
than all addicts (38% compared with 23%). Moreover, broken
marriages are almost as frequent as stable marriages among
all addicts, whereas among working addicts there are more than
twice as many stable as broken marriages.

The ethnic composition of the three samples can be seen from
Table 1.4.

Table 1.4

The Ethnic Composition of General Population,
Working Addicts, and All Addicts (in %)

Ethnicity	General population	Working addicts	All addicts
White	59	42	27
Black	26	40	50
Puerto Rican	15	18	23

These data confirm what is generally known: addiction is

largely an affliction of the minority groups. Thus blacks and
Puerto Ricans constitute 41% of the 17 to 49 year olds in Manhattan, Brooklyn, and the Bronx, but 73% of the addicts in the
city. Again the working addicts differ sharply from all addicts
and are more like the general population. Thus whites turn out
to be the largest group of working addicts, 42%, although they
make up only 27% of all addicts. Both blacks and Puerto Ricans
are underrepresented among the working addicts when compared
with all addicts. Addicts who work, as the data shown so far
clearly indicate, tend to fall between all addicts and the general
population. To be addicted and hold a job at the same time tends
to require people who are not too different from the normal population. Or put another way, an addict who can hold a job is
likely to be an addict who resembles the normal population in
many respects.

This same pattern appears in the final piece of information
which permits us to compare the three samples: education.
Educational attainment in the three groups is shown in Table 1.5.

Table 1.5

Educational Attainment of General Population,
Working Addicts, and All Addicts (in %)

Education	General population	Working addicts	All addicts
Less than high school graduate	43	52	68
High school graduate	33	28	23
Some college	24	20	9

The general population is much better educated than the addict
population. Thus two thirds of all addicts failed to graduate
from high school, compared with 43% of the general population.
And almost a quarter of the general population had some college
or more, compared with only 9% of all addicts. The working addicts, while not as well educated as the general population, are

better educated than all addicts, as almost half of them graduated
from high school and a fifth had some college experience. Thus
on education, too, working addicts are more like the normal population than addicts in general. Were an index of so-called typical traits constructed (for example, being a high school graduate,
being over 25, being married, and being white), it is clear that
the working addicts would score much higher than the total addict population.

There is one characteristic for which information is missing
on the general population but is available for both working addicts and addicts in general, and that is religion. These data
are shown in Table 1.6.

Table 1.6

The Religion of Working Addicts and All Addicts
(in %)

Religion	Working addicts	All addicts
Protestant	31	30
Catholic	57	51
Jew	6	3
Other	3	7
None	3	9

Catholics dominate the population of all addicts as well as the
working addicts. Information on the religious composition of
the city of New York is not readily available, but it is quite possible that Catholicism is now the majority religion in the city.
A decade or so ago it was estimated that New York had a Jewish
population of close to 40%. Even if the Jewish population of New
York has declined since then, it is obvious that Jews are heavily
underrepresented in the addict population. But nonetheless,
Jews are more prevalent among the working addicts than all
addicts. In fact, they are twice as likely to be found in this
group (6% compared with 3%). Thus even on the matter of religion, the working addicts look more like the general population
than do all addicts.

In view of the large number of blacks in the addict population and the tendency for blacks to be Protestants, the high concentration of Catholics among both working addicts and addicts in general is somewhat surprising. Among working addicts we can relate ethnicity to religion to find out the ethnic groups that are contributing the Catholics. This is done in Table 1.7.

Table 1.7

Ethnicity by Religion among Working Addicts
(in %)

Religion	Whites	Blacks	Puerto Ricans
Protestant	9	66	7
Catholic	75	23	92
Jew	15	—	—
Other	—	6	—
None	1	5	1

Table 1.7 shows that the Catholics who dominate the addict population come primarily from the Puerto Ricans and the whites. The Protestant working addicts are by and large blacks. If a white is Protestant, his chances are very slim of ending up in the addict population. That the white addicts were overwhelmingly Catholic suggests that drug abuse is a problem for the white ethnics who generally adhere to the Catholic religion.

The data presented in this chapter demonstrate that in every instance the social coloring of the working addicts departs from that of addicts in general and moves closer to that of the "normal" nonaddict population. The very fact that they held jobs makes the working addicts less deviant than addicts in general, and we now know that they were less deviant in other respects, having more of the social characteristics of the "normal" population.

On the basis of these findings we can now make safe inferences about the missing fourth group — working addicts who never entered treatment programs, the hidden addicts. Almost by defi-

nition, such persons might be viewed as successful addicts in
contrast with the failures we have sampled from treatment programs. Addicts who can support their habit, hold a full-time
job, and avoid treatment programs are probably not only successful as addicts but in the occupational world as well. As we
shall see in Chapter 7 of this report, most of the working addicts
we sampled were involved in a world of crime and in one way
or another ran into trouble that contributed to their ending up
in treatment programs. The hidden addicts, in contrast, are
likely to be people who earn so much money in their jobs or
careers that they do not have to resort to crime to support their
habit. We may conclude from the data already presented that
the hidden addicts are much more like the normal population
than the working addicts we sampled. They are undoubtedly
much more likely to be older, married, white, and well educated
than the working addicts we sampled. In fact, since whites were
the largest group among the working addicts we sampled (40%),
we can predict that whites make up a majority of the hidden addicts. In Chapter 3 we shall see that the working addicts had
occupations much like the general population, with one exception:
they are underrepresented among professionals, a group requir-
ing high education. Thus there were no doctors or lawyers,
engineers or architects in our sample of working addicts. But
other studies have shown that certain professions, notably medi-
cine, have relatively high rates of addiction. Addict doctors are
no doubt part of the unknown group of "hidden addicts," people
who so successfully blend their careers with their addiction that
they do not come to the attention of the authorities and do not
end up in treatment. We shall return to this theme in the concluding chapter. But we must now examine our sample of working addicts in some detail. How deeply were they into drugs and
to what kinds of drugs were they addicted and what kinds of jobs
did they hold? These matters concern us in the next several
chapters.

2

Drug History of Working Addicts

We know a good deal about the drug habits of the respondents in our sample, for example, the illegal drugs they used, the age when they were first addicted, the amount of money they spent maintaining their habit, and where they were located when they first realized that they were addicted. We begin this review of their drug history by considering this last datum. As we have seen, fully 75% of the working addicts were under 30 in 1974-75 when they were surveyed, and an equally large proportion were male. This means that a majority of the respondents were vulnerable to the draft during the Vietnam War. As a number of studies have shown, the soldiers who served in Vietnam were heavily exposed to easily accessible heroin, and a large number of them became addicted. We might suppose, then, that a substantial number of the respondents in this study first became addicts while serving in the military, especially in Vietnam. But in fact hardly any of them reported that they were in the military when they first became aware of their addiction. Only 12 of the 555 respondents, a mere 2%, so responded, and only half of this tiny group was in Vietnam. The great majority, 86%, were living in New York when they first realized that they were addicted, 2% were in Puerto Rico, and 10% in some other location.

The working addicts were asked how old they were when they realized that they were addicted to drugs, and they were also asked how old they were when they held their first full-time job. Thus we are in a position to determine the extent to which addiction preceded employment and the extent to which it followed upon employment. It turns out that 15% of these working addicts were addicted to drugs by the time they had reached the age of 15. The earliest addict in the sample claimed that he was addicted by the time he was 10 years old, and three persons said they were addicted by the time they were 11, clear proof that even the very young are not immune from drug addiction. Some 26% of the working addicts became addicted when they were 16 or 17, and 28%, when they were 18 or 19 (this is the modal age for addiction). Thus by the age of 19 a substantial majority were addicts (69%). Sixteen percent became addicts when they were 20 or 22, and by the age of 21 the great majority were addicts. Thus only 10% became addicted between the ages of 22 and 24, and only 6% became addicts after their twenty-fifth birthday. These data on age of addiction confirm what innumerable other studies show: addiction is a problem of the young. If a person can reach the age of 25 free of drugs, then he runs almost no risk of becoming an addict.

How old were these working addicts when they first entered the labor force and found full-time employment? If they turned to drugs at a relatively early age, the data show that they turned to gainful employment at just as early an age. Thus 15% had held full-time jobs by the time they were 15 years of age; an additional 46% had their first full-time job when they were 16 or 17 years old, bringing the total employed by the age of 17 to 61%. Twenty-seven percent had their first job as 18 or 19 year olds, with the result that fully 88% of these working addicts found their first full-time job before they turned 20, and only 12% did not go to work until after turning 20. It is clear from the data on age of addiction and age of full-time employment that most of the people in the sample became addicted after they entered the labor force. This inference is confirmed by the cross tabulation of age of addiction and age of first employment. Only 23% of the sample of working addicts became addicts before they entered the labor force. Fifteen percent became addicts during the same year that they went to work full-time, and fully 61% became addicts after they entered the labor force. These data

thus provide one answer to the question of why addicts are able
to hold full-time jobs when they are addicted. For most of them
the work habit preceded the drug habit; they apparently assimi-
lated work habits to the point that they were able to maintain
them even after they became addicts.

Nature of Drug Abuse

Virtually all of the respondents in this survey were addicted
to heroin (93%). Only 39 people, 7% of the sample, were addicted
to some other drug that brought them to a treatment center. A
majority of the respondents were users of more than one illegal
drug. The second most popular drug, following heroin, was
marijuana, which 54% of the sample used regularly. Cocaine
was third in popularity, having been used by 45% of the working
addicts. Methadone was used by 30%, barbiturates by 29%, and
amphetamines by 17%. A query about other illegal drugs not
mentioned specifically in our question turned up 5% who used
psychedelics like LSD, 2% who used morphine, 1% who used
codeine, and 1% who used other barbiturates.

When marijuana, which is considered to be a soft drug, is
excluded, we find that 39% of the sample were users of a single
hard drug, 39% used two hard drugs, and 22% used three or more
hard drugs. We shall soon consider how the polydrug users differed from the single drug users. But first we consider drug
usage on the job.

Those who admitted using a particular drug while they were
employed were asked whether they used this drug during the
working day. Table 2.1 shows the frequency of use and frequency
of use on the job for each drug.

In every instance substantially fewer used illegal drugs during
the working day. But the fall-off varies sharply with the drug. Thus
the majority of heroin users, fully 71% of the sample, took heroin
during the working day. To employ a heroin addict is, in most instances, to bring illegal drugs to the work place. Or put another
way, the heroin addict is least successful in separating his habit
from his job. In contrast, cocaine and barbiturates show a sharp

Table 2.1

Frequency of Use and Use on Job of Particular Drugs
(in %)

Drug	Used	Used on job
Heroin	93	71
Marijuana	54	33
Cocaine	45	21
Street methadone	30	19
Barbiturates	29	16
Amphetamines	17	12
Other illegal drugs (morphine, codeine, psychedelics, etc.)	9	9

fall-off from use to use on the job. Fewer than half of the cocaine users used cocaine on the job, and only about half of the
barbiturate users used this drug at work. Amphetamines present a quite different picture. Although a drug low in popularity,
used by only 17% of the sample, amphetamines if used are likely
to be used at work, as the drop-off is quite slight, from 17% to
12%. In all, 82% of the sample reported using some hard drug
(excluding marijuana and alcohol) during the working day, and
18% claimed that they did not use drugs while at work.

The nonheroin users. As Table 2.1 indicates, 7% of the sample, 39 persons in all, came to drug treatment centers addicted
to drugs other than heroin. What drugs did these nonheroin
users use? It turns out that 16 of them were dependent on a
single drug, and 23 of them were multiple drug users. Seven of
them were addicted only to the familiar heroin substitute, methadone, which they obtained on the street. Four used only barbiturates, 3 used only cocaine, and 2 were dependent solely on
amphetamines. In addition to the 7 who used methadone exclu-
sively, another 4 used methadone in combination with some other
drug. By far the most common combination of drugs among the
nonheroin addicts was barbiturates and amphetamines. Fully
16 of the 23 multiple drug users not dependent on heroin were

using both uppers and downers, and in some instances other drugs as well. Cocaine was used in combination with other drugs by 7 of those not dependent on heroin.

Drug Involvement

The last item of information we have on the working addicts' drug habits is a measure of how heavily involved in illegal drugs they were, the amount of money they spent each day to maintain their habit. The range of responses was extremely large. Some 14% spent $10 or less a day on drugs, 32% spent between $11 and $25, an equal percent (32%) spent between $26 and $50 per day, and 22%, more than one in every five, spent more than $50 daily on drugs. Some (24) reported spending more than $100 a day on their drug habit.

These various dimensions of involvement with drugs turn out to be related to each other. Those who became addicted at an early age and who became addicted before they went to work might be thought of as more deeply committed to drugs than those who did not get addicted until they were older and who entered the world of work before they became enmeshed in the world of drugs. The other three dimensions are even more closely related to the notion of involvement with drugs. Thus those who use several illicit drugs are presumably deeper into the drug culture than those who use only one; those who cannot get through the work day without taking illegal drugs are presumably more dependent on drugs than those who can get through the day without drugs; and finally, those who spend a great deal on their habit undoubtedly have a much stronger habit than those who spend relatively little. Age of addiction is strongly related to becoming addicted prior to entering the world of work, and it is also related to the amount spent on drugs; but it is only weakly related to the other two attributes of involvement, the number of drugs used and dependency on drugs during the working day. These relationships are shown in Table 2.2.

Not surprisingly, those who were addicted at an early age, often before they were old enough to work, were more likely to turn to drugs before entering the world of work; and conversely,

Table 2.2

Age of Addiction by Addiction Relative to Labor Force
Participation, Cost of Drugs, Number of Drugs Used,
and Use of Drugs on the Job (in %)

Age of addiction relative to age of first job	Age of addiction			
	10-16	17-18	19-21	22 plus
Addicted before first job	57	23	6	3
Addicted same year	22	20	10	3
Addicted after first job	22	57	84	93
Cost of addiction				
Over $25 a day	63	53	55	41
Number of drugs				
Three or more	29	20	21	13
Use of drugs on the job				
Using on job	83	85	86	78
N =	(134)	(178)	(152)	(91)

those who were relatively old before becoming addicted were
much more likely to have been in the labor force before they
turned to drugs. Those addicted at an early age tend to have a
stronger habit than those addicted at later ages, as indicated by
the amount of money spent on drugs. Another indicator of drug
involvement — the number of drugs used — is also related to age of
addiction. Those who became addicted early were much more likely than the others to use at least three different illegal drugs on a
regular basis. But a third measure of drug involvement, using
drugs during the working day, is not related to age of addiction.
Both the earliest group and the latest group are slightly below the
middle groups with regard to frequency of drug use on the job.

The three dimensions of drug involvement that most directly
bear on this concept are, as noted, the amount spent on drugs,
the number of drugs used, and reliance on drugs during the
working day. These three dimensions are highly related to each
other, as can be seen from Table 2.3.

Table 2.3

The Relationships among Number of Drugs Used, Amount
Spent Daily on Drugs, and Use of Drugs at Work (in %)

	Number of drugs		
	1	2	3
Use drugs at work	74	84	96
Spend more than $20 per day	69	80	81
	N = (216)	(219)	(118)
	Amount spent on drugs		
	Under $20	$20-49	$50 plus
Use drugs at work	71	82	92
	N = (131)	(257)	(157)

The more drugs used, the more likely is the addict to use
drugs during the working day, and spending more on drugs each
day is associated with using two or three drugs rather than only
one. Finally, reliance on drugs during the working day steadily
increases with the amount spent on drugs (from a low of 71% to
a high of 92%). These three dimensions of drug involvement can
be combined into an index of this concept. The resulting distribution of cases is as follows:

Involvement with Drugs Index
(in %)

Low (score 0)	16
Medium (score 1)	63
High (score 2, 3)	21

N = (544)

The great majority of the addicts fall into the middle group
on this index of drug involvement (63%). Some 16% are in the
low category, and at the opposite extreme are 21% of the sample
in the high category. (Almost all of the cases in the high

category scored two, that is endorsed two of the three items;
hardly any manifested all three aspects of involvement.)

Social Correlates
of Drug Involvement

   Having identified five dimensions of drug involvement and
shown that they are related to each other, we now consider the
social correlates of the various dimensions and of the index
based on the summation of three of the dimensions. We begin
this analysis by considering the correlates of age of addiction.
   Age of addiction. The age at which these working addicts
first became addicted is related to a number of social characteristics such as current age, sex, religion, ethnicity, and education. These findings are presented in Table 2.4.

Table 2.4

Age of Addiction by Sex, Religion, Ethnicity,
Age, and Education (in %)

Age of addiction	A. Sex		B. Religion			C. Ethnicity		
	Male	Female	Prot.	Cath.	Jew	Puerto R.	White	Black
10-16	26	18	18	28	18	31	25	20
17-18	31	35	33	32	35	30	33	32
19-21	28	27	26	27	26	29	29	26
22 and over	15	21	23	13	21	11	13	22
N =	(413)	(142)	(174)	(316)	(34)	(98)	(228)	(220)

Age of addiction	D. Current age				E. Education		
	17-21	22-24	25-29	30 plus	Less than HS	HS grad	Some college
10-16	56	25	17	17	29	20	16
17-18	34	50	27	21	35	31	26
19-21	10	21	38	27	23	29	37
22 and over	—	4	18	35	13	20	21
N =	(71)	(141)	(203)	(140)	(292)	(153)	(109)

As part A of the table shows, men were more likely than wom-
en to turn to drugs at an early age, and part B shows that Catholics were more likely than either Protestants or Jews to become
addicts at an early age. But this religion factor is probably a
result of the ethnicity pattern, for as part C of the table shows,
Puerto Ricans especially and whites as well were more likely
than blacks to take up drugs when quite young, and almost all
Puerto Ricans and most of the whites, as we have seen, are
Catholics. Part D of Table 2.4 shows a strong relationship between age of addiction and current age. The critical finding is
shown by the top row of part D, showing the percent of early addicts by current age. The bottom row, showing the percent who
became addicts after the age of 21, is constrained by current
age. By definition, no addicts who are not yet 22 could have become addicts after the age of 21; hence the 0 entry in that cell.
The top row indicates that early addiction is much more prevalent among those currently under 24 than those over 24. At first
glance this might seem tautological, but the tautology only applies to late, not early, addiction. Thus it is quite conceivable
that the same proportion in the older groups, e.g., the 25-29
year olds and those over 30, became addicts at an early age as
in the younger groups (those between 22 and 24, and 17 and 21).
That the older addicts did not become addicted at an early age
as frequently as the younger addicts is thus a substantive finding, one of some interest. This pattern strongly suggests that
the life span of addiction is rather limited. Presumably, addicts
can cope with their habit only for a limited number of years before they find themselves in treatment programs. Thus older
addicts in treatment became addicts at a later age than the
younger addicts in treatment, for had they become addicts much
earlier, they would have ended up in treatment programs at a
much earlier age.

Part E of Table 2.4, showing the relationship between age of
addiction and education, demonstrates the heavy cost of addiction
to the life chances of the addict. Those who failed to complete
high school were much more likely to be early addicts than those
who had more education. Fully 58% of those who had some col-

lege did not become addicts until they were 19 years of age or
older, in contrast with 36% of those who failed to complete high
school. Early addiction is clearly a deterrent to education, the
vital channel for upward mobility.

Time of addiction relative to time of first job. Whether the
addict turned to drugs before he started working or only after
he entered the labor force is related to some of his social characteristics. It is strongly related to current age, with the
younger addicts much more likely to have become addicted before they went to work than the older addicts. It is also related
somewhat to sex and religion. These findings are shown in
Table 2.5.

Table 2.5

Time of Addiction Relative to Entrance in Labor Force
by Sex, Religion, and Current Age (in %)

Addiction relative to work	Sex		Religion			Age			
	Men	Women	Prot.	Cath.	Jew	17-21	22-24	25-29	30 plus
Before first job	26	16	24	22	29	32	26	21	19
Same year	14	18	13	15	18	30	18	12	9
After first job	60	66	63	63	53	38	56	67	72
N =	(413)	(142)	(174)	(316)	(34)	(71)	(141)	(203)	(140)

Men are somewhat more likely than women to turn to drugs
before entering the labor market, a finding linked to their becoming addicts at an earlier age. Oddly enough, the Jews are
more likely than the Protestants and Catholics to become addicted before or at the same time that they go to work, rather
than after they take a job. Becoming addicted before entering
the labor market is strongly related to age, just as age of addiction was strongly related to age. Behind these findings, as we
have suggested, is the limited life span of addiction outside
treatment programs. Older addicts tended to take up their habit

relatively late, almost always after they went to work; younger
addicts tended to take up their habit at an early age, generally
before they went to work. But both the older and younger addicts
were probably addicted for a similar number of years before
turning to treatment. Since we interviewed them only while in
treatment, the age findings follow from the assumption of a
limited life span of addiction prior to treatment.

Cost of drug habit. How much the addict spent each day to
maintain his habit shows only moderate relationships with some
of the addicts' social characteristics and no relationships with
others. For example, cost of drugs is not related to current
age or education but is slightly related to sex, with men paying
somewhat more on the average for drugs than women; to religion, with Jews tending to spend more than Protestants and
Catholics; and to ethnicity, with whites typically spending more
than blacks and Puerto Ricans. These findings are shown in
Table 2.6.

Table 2.6

Cost of Drug Habit by Sex, Religion, and Ethnicity
(in %)

Cost of drugs	Sex		Religion			Ethnicity		
	Male	Female	Prot.	Cath.	Jew	White	Black	P.R.
Spend $50	31	23	24	31	38	34	25	28

All of these findings can be explained at least in part by income. In the next chapter we shall see that men earned more
on the average than women, that Jews earned more than Protestants and Catholics, and that whites earned substantially more
than members of the minority groups; and not surprisingly, income is strongly related to the amount spent daily on drugs.

Number of drugs used. As we have noted, 39% of the sample
used only one hard drug (almost always heroin); an equal number
used two hard drugs, and 22% used three or more drugs. Is
polydrug use related to the addicts' social characteristics?

The answer is yes. Most of the social attributes we have considered are related to polydrug use. This is true for sex, age,
religion, education, and ethnicity, as can be seen in Table 2.7.

Table 2.7

Number of Drugs Used by Sex, Religion, Education,
Age, and Ethnicity (in %)

Number	Sex		Religion			Education		
of						Less		Some
drugs	Male	Female	Prot.	Cath.	Jew	HSG	HSG	coll.
One	37	46	43	40	23	42	37	34
Two	40	37	46	33	50	41	36	43
Three plus	23	17	11	27	27	17	27	23
N =	(413)	(142)	(174)	(316)	(34)	(292)	(153)	(109)

Number	Age				Ethnicity		
of				30			Puerto
drugs	17-21	22-24	25-29	plus	White	Black	Rican
One	27	34	43	45	31	43	50
Two	35	44	38	40	33	46	37
Three plus	38	22	19	15	36	10	12
N =	(71)	(141)	(203)	(140)	(228)	(220)	(98)

The three social characteristics shown in the top part of
Table 2.7, sex, religion, and education, have only moderate relationships with number of drugs used. The sex difference is
rather slight, as is the difference among the three levels of education; the religious differences are sharper since Jews are
much more likely than Protestants and Catholics to use more
than one drug. The sharpest differences are found for the two
characteristics in the second half of the table, age and ethnicity.
Use of multiple drugs steadily increases as age declines, and
whites are much more likely than blacks and Puerto Ricans to
use more than one drug. In fact, the modal response for Puerto
Ricans is one drug, for blacks the mode is two drugs, and for
the whites it is three drugs.

The final dimension of drug involvement is dependence on drugs during the working day. We have seen that the great majority of these working addicts, all but 18%, did take illegal drugs while on the job. Using drugs during the working day is slightly related to education and sex and strongly related to religion and ethnicity. Again, the Jews and the whites among these working addicts demonstrate greater involvement with drugs, as can be seen from Table 2.8.

Table 2.8

Use of Drugs on the Job by Sex, Education,
Religion, and Ethnicity (in %)

Use of drugs on job	Sex		Education		
	Men	Women	Less than HSG	HSG	Some college
Use on job	84	78	78	86	86

Use of drugs on job	Religion			Ethnicity		
	Prot.	Cath.	Jew	White	Black	Puerto Rican
Use on job	73	85	94	93	74	75

The sex and education relationships are slight, but the religion and ethnicity patterns are quite pronounced. Just as was true for cost of drugs and number of drugs used, so we now find that Jews and whites, in contrast with non-Jews and nonwhites, are much more dependent on drugs during the course of the working day. These three dimensions bear directly on drug involvement, and it is clear from the findings that Jews and whites among these working addicts were more deeply involved in drugs than their counterparts. One hypothesis to explain these findings is that Jewish and white addicts were better able than their counterparts to adjust to the world of work. As a result of their better adjustment, according to this theory, they could indulge their drug habit to a greater degree without endangering their employment. In the next chapter we shall examine a number of dimensions of participation in the labor force, including occupation and income, that bear on this hypothesis.

Index of drug involvement. We have seen that the various dimensions of drug involvement are related to sex, religion, education, age, and ethnicity. It should follow then that the index of drug involvement, based on number of drugs, cost of drugs, and use of drugs on the job, is also related to these social characteristics. By and large this assumption is correct, with some modifications. For example, men and women do not differ much on the drug involvement index, since 22% of the men, compared with 17% of the women, scored high. And drug involvement proves to be curvilinearly related to education, with those who failed to complete high school least involved (17% high), the high school graduates most involved (27% high), and those who had at least some college in the middle (24% in the high-involvement category). But religion, and especially age and ethnicity, are related to drug involvement, with Protestants much lower on involvement than Catholics and Jews, the young much more involved than the older addicts, and whites much more involved than either blacks or Puerto Ricans. These relationships are shown in Table 2.9.

Table 2.9

Drug Involvement by Religion, Age, and Ethnicity (in %)

Religion	Low	Medium	High	N
Protestant	25	64	11	(174)
Catholic	13	61	26	(316)
Jew	6	68	27	(34)
Age				
17-21	16	55	28	(134)
22-24	15	65	20	(178)
25-29	13	66	21	(151)
30 plus	21	67	12	(91)
Ethnicity				
White	5	60	35	(228)
Black	24	66	10	(219)
Puerto Rican	25	64	11	(98)

Jews are much less likely than Protestants to be in the low-involvement category, with Catholics in between, and they are much more likely than Protestants to be in the high group. The percentage of high-involvement cases steadily declines with age (from 28 to 12%), and the white addicts are more than three times as likely as the black and Puerto Rican addicts to be in the category of high involvement with drugs. In the next chapter we examine the work history of these addicts, and we shall discover some of the resources that permit the whites to be highly involved with drugs.

3

Work History of Working Addicts

We have seen that fully 61% of the working addicts held a full-time job by the time they turned 17, and that a majority entered the labor market before they became addicted to drugs. We now consider the kinds of jobs they had, the industries in which they were employed, the amount of money they earned, and various attributes of their jobs.

The respondents were asked how many full-time jobs they had held. In keeping with the notion of instability as characteristic of the addict's life, these working addicts held a number of different jobs during their career in the job market. Only 8% had but one full-time job during their work history. Some 32% had two or three jobs; 26% had four or five, and fully 32% reported that they had held six or more full-time jobs during their relatively brief periods in the labor market. Were comparable data available on nonaddicts of the same ages, we would undoubtedly find that nonaddicts had much less job turnover.

Labor Force Participation of Working Addicts

We begin this portrait of the work history of these addicts by noting where they ended up in the job world, that is, the kinds of occupations they had, the industries in which they worked, and how successful they were in the world of work as measured by income.

Table 3.1 shows the kinds of jobs these working addicts held

when they first entered the labor force and the kinds of jobs
they worked on longest while addicted.

Table 3.1

Occupations of Working Addicts for First Job and
Longest Job Held When Addicted

Occupation	First job		Longest job	
Higher white collar	N	%	N	%
Professional, technical,				
and kindred	4		4	
Managers and administrators	4		10	
Community service workers	11		14	
Medical paraprofessionals	10		17	
	29	5	45	8
Lower white collar				
Sales workers	50		40	
Clerical and kindred	145		134	
	195	36	174	32
Skilled craftsmen	50	9	61	11
Semiskilled				
Operatives, transportation				
operators	82		113	
Maintenance workers	17		20	
Uniformed city employees	7		6	
Private security guards	5		8	
	111	21	147	26
Unskilled and low level service				
Laborers	65		61	
Personal service	90		64	
	155	29	125	23

In setting up this classification, we have stretched somewhat
the traditional meaning of higher white collar by including in
this category medical paraprofessionals, such as nurses' aides
and community service workers, a group that includes counselors

in drug programs, teacher's aides, and social workers. The
category of "personal service," which we have grouped with
laborers in the unskilled category, includes restaurant workers,
beauticians, messengers, and laundry workers.

Even with a most liberal definition of higher white-collar occupations, we find that only a tiny fraction of the working addicts
had such jobs. Almost all the working addicts fall into three
broad job categories, lower white collar, semiskilled blue collar, and unskilled blue collar. By comparing the results for
first job and for job held longest while addicted, we learn that
these working addicts achieved a certain amount of upward mobility in their work careers. Thus the number in higher white-
collar occupations increases, as does the number of skilled
craftsmen and semiskilled workers, while the number in the
relatively unskilled lower white-collar jobs and unskilled blue-
collar jobs declines from first job to longest job. Table 3.1
shows that in terms of the job they held longest, the working
addicts were employed in a wide range of occupations. A few
had professional, managerial, or administrative jobs, about a
third worked in lower white-collar jobs, more than a third were
employed as skilled or semiskilled workers, and about a quarter
were in the rather lowly occupations of laborers and low-level
personal service workers.

It is of some interest to compare the longest jobs held by
these working addicts with the occupations of those of comparable age, i.e., 17 to 49, of the residents of three boroughs in
which these addicts were located, Manhattan, the Bronx, and
Brooklyn.

Table 3.2 shows the occupational distribution of this age group
in the general population of these boroughs according to the 1970
census and the occupations of our sample of addicts.

When the occupations of the working addicts are compared
with the general population of comparable age, we find some
sharp differences and some similarities. Lower white-collar
workers (sales and clerical) are present in both samples to the
same degree, and the percentage of unskilled workers and service employees is also quite similar in the two groups. But the

Table 3.2

Longest Occupation of Working Addicts Compared with
Occupations of General Population of Comparable Age
in 1970 Census (in %)

Occupation	Working addicts	General population
Higher white collar	8	20
Lower white collar	32	31
Craftsmen	11	7
Semiskilled	26	14
Laborers and service	23	28

working addicts were much more likely to be employed as
skilled craftsmen and semiskilled operatives and transportation
workers than their counterparts in the general population, and
much less likely to be employed as professionals, managers,
and administrators, that is, in higher white-collar occupations.
Had we a more stringent definition of higher white collar, one
that would exclude paraprofessionals, this discrepancy would
be even greater. A major reason for the exclusion of working
addicts from higher white-collar occupations is their relatively
low level of education. As we saw in Chapter 1, more than half
the addicts failed to complete high school, only 20% had some
college experience, and only 1% graduated from college. In contrast, 24% of the general population had some college, and 12%
had graduated from college. Although the working addicts were
less likely to make it to the top of the occupational hierarchy
than the general population, they were by no means doomed to
the bottom of the occupational structure because of their habit.
As Table 3.2 shows, they were somewhat less likely to be in the
lowest category (laborers and service) than the general population and more likely than the general population to be at the top
of the blue-collar world as skilled craftsmen. Addiction, contrary to popular opinion, does not preclude addicts from obtaining fairly decent jobs; and with the exception of the highest

category of professionals and managers, the addicts compare
rather well with the general population in the kinds of jobs they
had.

We not only know the main occupation of the working addicts,
but we also know the type of industry in which they were employed. Some of them worked in the public sector as employees
of the local, state, or federal government; most of them worked
in the private sector, and we have divided the private sector into two basic categories — white-collar industries and blue collar, a distinction based on the kinds of jobs that the bulk of the
labor force in the industry have. In terms of these very broad
categories, we find that 6% of the working addicts were employed
by government, 41% worked in white-collar industries, and 53%
in what we classified as blue-collar industries. Table 3.3 shows
the distribution of cases in the various white-collar industries.

Table 3.3

White-collar Industries in Which Addicts Were Employed

Industry	N	%
Retailing	90	17
Publishing, printing	24	4
Hospitals	23	4
Finance: banks, brokerage houses	21	4
Entertainment	18	3
Wholesalers-distributors	16	3
Welfare: community service	14	3
White-collar services	10	2
Insurance	6	1
Advertising	1	*
	223	41

Hospitals are included in the white-collar group because almost all of the addicts who worked in hospitals had paraprofes-
sional jobs. Community service agencies include day care centers and drug treatment programs, and white-collar services

is a classification we developed to cover such diverse services as accounting and law firms, credit investigators, market research firms, laboratories, and exhibitors. As can be seen from Table 3.3, retailing is the industry that employed by far the largest number of these working addicts; retailing leads all the industries, including the blue-collar ones shown in the next table. Surveys of the public at large have shown that salesmen, of all occupational groups, are most susceptible to drug abuse, and Table 3.1 showed that the largest number of addicts were employed as clerical and sales workers. The dominance of retailing over all other industries in the employment of addicts is in keeping with these earlier findings. Publishing, hospitals, and finance institutions are virtually tied for a rather distant second place behind retailing. The entertainment world has long been associated with illicit drugs, and a fair number of the addicts in our sample had been employed in entertainment.

A certain degree of caution must be applied in interpreting Table 3.3. Although other studies have documented that those employed in retailing are prone to drug abuse, it would be a mistake to assume that these data reflect accurately the relative frequency of drug use in the various industries. These data refer only to the people we interviewed in treatment programs, and they may or may not be representative of the world of work. One reason for such caution is suggested by the fact that the advertising industry is represented in Table 3.3 by only a single case. Our study of firms in different industries disclosed that our informants in advertising agencies reported a relatively high amount of drug use by their employees, mainly their professional employees. But addicts in the higher reaches of the occupational structure have considerable resources that they can call on and thus are likely to avoid the kinds of treatment programs from which we sampled our respondents.

The blue-collar industries represented in our sample are shown in Table 3.4.

Just as retailing led all other white-collar industries, so manufacturing leads all blue-collar industries. In second place is a category that requires some explanation: personal services

Table 3.4

Blue-collar Industries in Which Addicts Were Employed

Industry	N	%
Manufacturing	85	15
Personal services	57	10
Construction	39	7
Real estate maintenance	38	7
Restaurants	26	5
Freight transportation	21	4
Utilities	19	4
Merchant seamen, longshoremen	4	1
	289	53

more akin to the blue-collar than white-collar world. Under
this rubric we have grouped such firms as dry cleaning and
laundry establishments, messenger services, security agencies,
parking lots, taxi companies, barber shops and beauty parlors,
hotels, baby-sitting services, and pet establishments. The construction industry and what we call real estate maintenance
share third place among these blue-collar industries. The real
estate maintenance category encompasses doormen, janitors,
window cleaners, and house painters. Restaurants could easily
have been grouped with personal services, but so many of the
addicts were employed by restaurants that we have kept them a
separate category. The category freight transportation consists
mainly of truck drivers, and some 21 members of the sample
were employed in this industry. New York City has only two
major utilities, the telephone company and the gas and electric
company, both of which have extremely large work forces. As
Table 3.4 shows, 19 of the addicts sampled had been employed
by these companies. Just as the occupational distribution showed
a fairly broad spread of the addicts through the occupational
structure, so the data of Tables 3.3 and 3.4 reveal a rather
broad spread through the spectrum of industries.

A critical question that the data on occupation and industry

leave unanswered is whether certain jobs and industries attract
those who are addicted or whether there is something about the
work these people did that led them to experiment with drugs.
We have seen that the great majority of the sample entered the
work force before they were addicted, which leaves open the
possibility that there was something about their work that turned
them on to drugs. The two leading industries with respect
to drug abuse according to these data are retailing and manufacturing. Retailing involves a high degree of interaction
with other people, including the idea of "selling" oneself
to others. It is conceivable that such employment would
lead people to seek mood-manipulating drugs. Manufacturing, in contrast, tends to involve dull, repetitive work, the
kind of work that requires considerable effort to get through
each day. It may well be that mood-manipulating drugs are
also needed by many in this kind of work. In short, the
findings of Table 3.3 and 3.4 are suggestive of hypotheses
that might be tested by some of the data on hand and by
further research.

The majority of the working addicts, as we have seen, were
employed in blue-collar industries in occupations toward the
bottom of the job hierarchy. It is perhaps not surprising, then,
that a majority of the addicts had incomes well under $10,000
a year. The distribution of cases according to income is shown
in Table 3.5.

Table 3.5

Income of the Working Addicts

Weekly wages	Yearly income	%
Under $100	Under $5,200	19
$100-149	$5,200-7,750	40
$150-199	$7,800-10,350	22
$200-249	$10,400-12,950	9
$250 and over	$13,000 and over	10

Almost a fifth of the addicts were in the lowest income category, earning less than $100 a week, and two fifths earned between $100 and $149 a week. In all, 59% of the addicts earned less than $8,000 a year. At the other extreme we find 19% who earned over $10,000 a year, including 10% who earned over $13,000 a year, a figure that places them well into the middle class.

Although most working addicts had rather small incomes, there were a few who did quite well financially. In all, some 16 persons in the sample earned more than $350 a week, or more than $18,000 a year, while they were addicted to drugs. It is of some interest to take a closer look at these relatively affluent addicts.

Eight of these high earning addicts, half of the total, were construction workers, a testimonial to the high salaries of that industry; three of them owned their own business, two were musicians, one was a parking lot attendant, one was a staff accountant for a law firm, and one worked as a carpet layer. The mean salary of the construction workers was $405 a week. One of the three businessmen owned a bar and night club, and he earned $1,150 a week, or more than $50,000 a year, which made him the highest paid person in the sample. Another businessman owned a poodle-grooming shop, and he earned $500 a week; and the third businessman owned a dry cleaning establishment and earned $400 a week. One of the two musicians had earned $850 a week, and the other $356 a week. The parking lot attendant earned $500 a week, and the law firm accountant and carpet layer made $370 and $350, respectively.

Whites dominated this elite group of addicts, with eleven of them white, three black, one Puerto Rican, and one American Indian. They were predominantly Catholic, fourteen, compared with one Protestant and one Jew. All of these high-earning addicts were men, and their ages ranged from 20 to 37, with an average age of 28. Their education was somewhat above average for the sample. Seven had failed to complete high school, five were high school graduates, and four had some college. Four of these high earners still had their jobs when they were interviewed (they were enrolled in methadone maintenance programs); six of the men in the group were forced to leave their jobs because of their drug habit, four (construction workers) had been laid off, and only two had voluntarily left their jobs.

Of special significance is the fact that in spite of their high earnings, most of these addicts were unable to support their habit on the basis of their earnings alone. Thirteen of the sixteen supplemented their income in some way, and twelve of them admitted to criminal acts, particularly stealing or dealing in drugs as ways of adding to their income.

All of these high earners were heroin addicts, almost all, fifteen of sixteen, used drugs during the working day, and fourteen of them were using other illegal drugs in addition to heroin on a daily basis. In short, these financially well off addicts were on the average more deeply involved with drugs than the rest of the sample.

It is difficult to tell how the earnings of these addicts compare with the general population in this time period of 1974-75. When compared with those of comparable age in the 1970 census, these addicts appear to have made out rather well. Of course, the level of income was lower in 1970 than in 1974 and 1975, but precisely how much lower is difficult to estimate. In any case the addicts reported incomes in 1974 and 1975 that were substantially higher than those of their counterparts in Manhattan, Brooklyn, and the Bronx in 1970. Since the working addicts are mostly males, we compare the salaries of the male addicts in our sample as of 1974-75 with the earnings of men between the ages of 17 and 49 in these boroughs of New York City in 1970 (see Table 3.6).

As these data show, 24% of the male working addicts had incomes in excess of $10,000, compared with 18% of the men of comparable age in the general population in 1970. Given the fairly sharp rise in earnings between 1970 and 1975, it is quite likely that the poorly paid group in the general population shrunk a great deal and the well paid group increased substantially. One might guess that by 1975 the proportion earning over $10,000 in the general population even exceeded the proportion in the

Table 3.6

Income of Male Addicts (1974-75) and of Males 17-49
in the General Population (Manhattan, Bronx, and Brooklyn)
in 1970 (in %)

Income	Male addicts (1974-75)	General population
Under $5,000	15	41
$5,000-7,799	36	24
$7,800-10,399	25	18
$10,000-12,999	11	7
$13,000 and over	13	11

sample of working addicts. But clearly, Table 3.6 suggests that
the working addicts did rather well in the market place compared
with the general population. If their earnings were not equal to
those of the general population, it is highly doubtful that they
were far behind, and for all we know, they may even have been
ahead, as the comparison with five-year-old data suggests.

There is one respect, however, in which the income data on
these working addicts does differ from the general population.
In general, income varies with occupational prestige, with
higher-ranking occupations being associated with higher income
than lower-ranking ones. But this is not at all the case in this
sample of working addicts. In fact there are just as many people in the lowest occupational category (lower-level service and
laborers) who earned over $200 a week (23%) as in the higher
white-collar group (22%). The occupational category with the
highest income turns out to be craftsmen, with 31% earning over
$200 a week; and the category with the lowest income is lower
white collar (clerical and sales), with only 8% earning over $200
a week.

Social Correlates of Labor Force Participation

What kinds of people in this addict sample managed to obtain
relatively high-status jobs, what kinds worked in white-collar

industries, and what kinds earned fairly high incomes? A number of social characteristics were found to be related to type of occupation: sex, education, religion, and ethnicity. Women were much more likely than men to have had white-collar jobs, primarily sales and clerical jobs; the better-educated addicts tended to have higher-status jobs; Jews were more likely to have white-collar jobs than either Protestants or Catholics; and oddly enough, Puerto Ricans were more likely to have white-collar jobs than either whites or blacks. These findings are shown in Table 3.7.

Table 3.7

Occupation by Sex, Education, Religion, and Ethnicity
(in %)

Occupation	Sex		Education		
	Men	Women	Less than HSG	HSG	Some college
Higher white collar	7	11	5	9	15
Lower white collar	22	59	25	38	40
Craftsmen	14	3	11	11	10
Operators, transit, maintenance	31	14	30	22	25
Lower service and laborers	26	13	29	20	10
N =	(408)	(142)	(292)	(152)	(108)

Occupation	Religion			Ethnicity		
	Prot.	Cath.	Jew	White	Black	Puerto Rican
Higher white collar	8	8	12	8	9	7
Lower white collar	31	31	44	29	31	38
Craftsmen	10	12	9	13	7	12
Operators, transit, maintenance	26	27	21	27	26	27
Lower service and laborers	25	21	15	22	27	16
N =	(173)	(314)	(34)	(227)	(219)	(97)

As Table 3.7 shows, women addicts were concentrated in
lower white-collar jobs, but they were also more likely than
men to have higher white-collar jobs (paraprofessionals were
included in the higher white-collar group), with the result that
women were more than three times as likely as men to be in
the white-collar group. The better educated were much more
likely than the poorly educated to be in both white-collar groups,
and the poorly educated were more prevalent on the lower rungs
of the occupational ladder. Fully 59% of the Jews had white-
collar occupations, compared with 39% of the Protestants and
Catholics. But as the data on ethnicity show, there is relatively
little difference among whites, blacks, and Puerto Ricans with
regard to the occupations they had. Puerto Ricans are somewhat more likely than either blacks or whites to have had lower
white-collar occupations, and the occupational distributions of
whites and blacks are quite similar.

Industry of employment is also related to some of the social
characteristics of the addicts. Thus women were somewhat
more likely than the men to work in white-collar industries
(48% compared with 39%). Again, we find Puerto Ricans more
likely to be employed in white-collar industries, whatever their
occupation, than whites and blacks (53% compared with 40% and
38%, respectively, of whites and blacks). Jews were more likely
than Protestants and Catholics to be employed in white-collar
industries, and those who had some college were also more
likely to have worked in white-collar industries than those of
lesser education. Education turns out to be particularly important for public employment. Only 5% of those who failed to
finish high school worked for government, and 6% of those who
graduated from high school. In contrast, 12% of those who had
some college — at least twice as many — worked for government.

How much money the working addicts earned turns out to be
strongly related to their social characteristics. The male addicts earned much more on the average than the female addicts,
the better educated earned more than the poorly educated, and
Jews earned more than Protestants and Catholics. But the
sharpest differences were found for ethnicity. The white addicts

earned much more than the black and Puerto Rican addicts. These findings are shown in Table 3.8.

Table 3.8

Income of Working Addicts by Sex, Education Religion, and Ethnicity (in %)

Weekly income	Sex		Education		
	Men	Women	Less than HS	HS grad.	Some college
Under $100	15	29	22	20	9
$100-149	36	50	42	38	37
$150-199	25	16	17	25	30
$200-249	11	4	9	7	12
$250 and over	13	1	10	10	12
N =	(410)	(140)	(292)	(153)	(109)

Weekly income	Religion			Ethnicity		
	Prot.	Cath.	Jew	White	Black	Puerto Rican
Under $100	28	14	12	12	25	24
$100-149	48	36	29	28	50	44
$150-199	15	26	24	27	15	24
$200-249	4	11	18	16	5	4
$250 and over	5	13	17	17	5	4
N =	(173)	(314)	(34)	(225)	(220)	(98)

As Table 3.8 shows, about half the men, but only one fifth of the women, earned over $7,800 a year; and men were almost five times as likely as women to earn over $10,000 a year. Education also is related to income, as 36% of the most poorly educated, 42% in the middle, and 54% in the high-education group earned over $7,800 a year. Oddly enough, though, education is not particularly significant for earning a high income. Thus those who failed to complete high school are as likely as high school graduates to earn over $10,000, and those who went to college do only a little better in this high-income group than those who did not complete high school. (Earning over $200 a week were 19% of those who did not graduate from high school, 17% of the high school graduates, and 24% of those who had some college.) The Jewish addicts earned substantially more than the Protestant and Catholic addicts, as 35% of them had incomes over $10,000, compared with 24% of the Catholics and only 9% of the Protestants. But this religious finding is largely a result of ethnicity, for as we have seen, the Catholics were mainly white and the Protestants mainly black. The ethnic pattern shows that the white addicts earned much more than the black and Puerto Rican addicts and that Puerto Ricans did somewhat better than the blacks. Thus only 40% of the whites earned less than $7,800, compared with 68% of the Puerto Ricans and fully 75% of the blacks. And in the highest income group, those earning over $250 a week, we find more than three times as many whites as blacks and Puerto Ricans (17% compared with 5% and 4%).

Earlier we noted that whites were highly overrepresented among working addicts, and now we see that even in this elite group of addicts, whites do much better financially than do minority group addicts. The greater involvement of white addicts in the world of work and their greater financial rewards for working suggest that white addicts, perhaps because they belong to the dominant group, are better able than minority group addicts to integrate the deviant world of drugs with the normal world of work. The implications of this finding are rather profound. It may well turn out that drug addiction is the devastating social problem that it is not so much because of the debilitating effects of drugs on the users but because so many of those who use drugs are otherwise socially handicapped by virtue of belonging to minority groups that suffer from discrimination. Were addiction limited only to whites, the social costs might well be less, as white addicts appear to better adjust to normal life than minority addicts.

We have seen that most addicts had a number of full-time jobs

during their relatively brief period in the labor market, and we
interpreted this finding as suggesting a rather high degree of
job instability for addicts. But we have more direct information
on the addicts' ability to hold a job. The addicts were asked
what was the length of their longest held job while they were addicted. There was considerable variation in the responses to
this question. Some addicts, 11% in all, were unable to hold a
job for longer than five months. And another 20% held their jobs
from 6 months to 11 months, that is, 31% of the addicts worked
on the same job for less than a year. Another 25% held their job
for 12 to 23 months, 15% for 24 to 35 months, and fully 30% of
the addicts managed to hold the same job for three or more
years. That 41% of the addicts held their job for two or more
years, and a substantial number for three or more years while
addicted, indicates that many addicts are able to adjust rather
well to the world of work. The popular myth of addicts behaving
in such erratic ways that they cannot participate in the structured
world of work is in need of serious qualification. Many addicts
apparently are able to hold steady jobs stretching over several
years while they are addicted.

Upon analysis it turns out that certain kinds of addicts were
more successful than others in holding their jobs for long periods of time. Length of employment steadily increases with the
age of the addict. Thus only 12% of the addicts under 21 held
the same job for two or more years, a figure that climbs to 32%
for addicts between the ages of 22 and 24, to 45% for addicts between the ages of 25 and 29, and 58% of the addicts over 30. Men
did better than women in holding their job, as did the better educated when compared with the poorly educated. Religion is also
a factor, with Jews holding their jobs longer on the average than
Protestants and Catholics; and finally, ethnicity is related to
length of job, with whites keeping their jobs for a longer period
than the blacks. These relationships are shown in Table 3.9.

Of all the associations shown in Table 3.9, by far the strongest
is that between length of employment and age. Older addicts,
presumably more experienced in managing their drug habit, had
little difficulty holding their jobs for substantial periods of time.

Table 3.9

Length of Longest Job by Sex, Age, Education, Religion, and Ethnicity (in %)

Length of longest job	Sex		Age				Education		
	Men	Women	17-21	22-24	25-29	30+	LHS	HSG	Some coll.
Under 1 year	29	36	57	39	25	17	36	29	16
1-2 years	23	31	22	26	27	22	24	24	28
2-3 years	15	13	12	16	14	16	12	17	20
3 years plus	34	20	9	19	35	45	28	30	36
N =	(357)	(132)	(69)	(153)	(196)	(136)	(281)	(147)	(106)

Length of longest job	Religion			Ethnicity		
	Prot.	Cath.	Jew	White	Black	Puerto Rican
Under 1 year	38	27	16	21	42	25
1-2 years	24	25	22	26	24	25
2-3 years	11	15	28	16	12	18
3 years plus	28	33	34	37	22	32
N =	(166)	(305)	(32)	(219)	(213)	(93)

Education is also fairly strongly related to length of job, a finding that is even more impressive when it is kept in mind that
the older addicts, who tended to keep their jobs for a long time,
tend to be more poorly educated than the younger addicts. Were
age held constant, the education finding would be even stronger.
Blacks are not nearly as likely as whites to have kept their jobs
for at least two years (31% compared with 49%), a further indication
of the greater difficulty blacks have than whites in integrating the
world of work with their drug habit. Again, the Puerto Ricans are
very close to the whites on this dimension of work.

Characteristics of the Longest Job
_____

Apart from the various dimensions of what we have called
"labor force participation" (occupation, industry, income, number of jobs, and length of longest job), we know a good deal about
the nature of the jobs the working addicts had. We know, for
example, whether the work involved hard physical labor, whether
the work was dirty, and whether the job was dangerous, factors
which can be considered as measures of how "strenuous" the
job was. We also know how much autonomy the worker had,
whether he found the job interesting, how good his chances for
promotion were, and how much he liked his job, all measures
of job quality or job satisfaction.

The large number of addicts employed in blue-collar work is
suggested by the fact that fully 42% answered affirmatively when
asked whether the job they held for the longest time involved
"hard physical work." Even more, 47%, responded affirmatively
when asked whether the work they did required them to get dirty,
and 38% answered yes when asked whether the work they did was
"dangerous in any way." These three attributes are highly related to each other, meaning that jobs that involved any one of
them were likely to involve the other two. They can be taken as
measures of what might be called "strenuousness of work." An
index of this concept based on the three attributes of "hard physical work," job requires "getting dirty," and job is "dangerous"
yields the following distribution of cases:

Strenuousness of Work Index

Score	%
Low (0)	40
Medium low (1)	16
Medium high (2)	19
High (3)	25
N =	(550)

Fully 40% of the sample had jobs that were totally free of the symptoms of strenuous work. The jobs of 16% involved one of the three items, the jobs of 19% involved two of the items that measure strenuous work, and finally, 25% held jobs that placed them in the highest category of strenuous work, with all three indicators present. Later on, when we come to consider the correlates of this index, we shall combine the two high groups into a category containing 44% of the cases.

The measures of the quality of the job that the working addicts held include the following question: "Did you decide how to do your work or did you follow closely orders from other people?" Somewhat surprisingly, a substantial majority, 61%, said that they decided for themselves what to do, a degree of autonomy not generally associated with semiskilled and unskilled blue-collar work. When asked about their chances for promotion on the job they held longest, some 39% said their chances were very good, 26% said fairly good, and only 34% reported that their changes were not good. Combining the "very good" and "fairly good" categories, we find that 65% of the working addicts rated their jobs favorably from the viewpoint of advancement. Yet another measure of the quality of the job is provided by the responses to a question that asked: "Did you find the work you did interesting, dull, or in between?" Again, a clear majority rated their jobs favorably, as 60% said they found their jobs "interesting" rather than "dull" or "in between." Finally, when asked directly how much they liked their job, 58% reported that they "liked it a lot," 34% said they "liked it a little," and only 7% claimed that they "hated it." It turns out that these various attributes of the quality of job are all related to each other,

permitting us to combine them into an index of job quality, or
to use a more common phrase, "job satisfaction." The distribution of the sample of working addicts on this index is as follows:

Job Quality or Satisfaction	
Score	%
Very low (0)	13
Low (1)	21
Medium (2)	19
High (3)	27
Very high (4)	20

The distribution is skewed toward the high satisfaction end of
the continuum. A fifth of the addicts rated their jobs favorably
in all four respects, and 47% rated it favorably in at least three
of four respects. At the other extreme, only 13% of the sample
had nothing good to say about their jobs, and another 21% rated
their jobs favorably on only one of the four dimensions. For
purposes of subsequent analysis we shall split this distribution
into a low category (scores 0, 1 and 2), representing 53% of the
cases, and a high category (scores 3 and 4), with 47% of the
cases.

One might suppose that strenuous work is less desirable than
nonstrenuous work that is not dangerous, does not involve physical labor, and does not require getting dirty. But among these
working addicts there is no relationship at all between these
two attributes, since 56% of those with less strenuous jobs
scored high on satisfaction, and an identical proportion of those
in more strenuous jobs received the same score. Both indices
are related to certain labor force participation variables and to
certain social characteristics. Table 3.10 shows how strenuousness of work and job satisfaction are related to occupation.

Reading down the first column, we see that strenuous work is
rarely found in white-collar occupations but dominates blue-
collar jobs. Fully two thirds of the working addicts who were
employed as craftsmen and lower level service workers and
laborers scored high on this index. Job satisfaction is most

Table 3.10

Strenuousness of Work and Job Satisfaction by Occupation

Occupation	High strenuousness of work		High job satisfaction	
	%	N	%	N
Higher white collar	11	(45)	67	(45)
Lower white collar	13	(174)	45	(174)
Craftsmen	66	(61)	60	(61)
Operator, transit, maintenance	60	(147)	42	(147)
Lower service, laborers	67	(125)	39	(125)

prevalent among the relatively few addicts employed in higher white-collar occupations and is almost as high among those employed as craftsmen. In contrast, job satisfaction is rather low among lower white-collar workers, the semiskilled blue-collar workers, and the unskilled blue-collar workers. That the lower level white-collar workers are only slightly more satisfied with their jobs than the semiskilled and unskilled workers is in keeping with the earlier finding that they were the least well paid occupational group. Table 3.11 shows how income is related to strenuousness of work and job satisfaction among these working addicts.

Table 3.11

Strenuousness of Work and Job Satisfaction by Income

Weekly wages	High strenuousness of work		High job satisfaction	
	%	N	%	N
Under $100	31	(105)	25	(105)
$100-149	41	(220)	39	(220)
$150-199	44	(122)	59	(122)
$200-249	56	(50)	68	(50)
$250 and over	66	(56)	69	(56)

The second column demonstrates a very strong relationship between income and job satisfaction. Not surprisingly, satisfaction steadily increases with income. More surprising is the strong positive relationship between strenuousness of work and income. The more strenuous jobs, those found among the various blue-collar workers, especially craftsmen, pay much better than the less strenuous jobs, such as clerks and salesmen. Earlier we saw that the various categories of occupations did vary sharply in income. Semiskilled and unskilled workers and higher white-collar workers had similar incomes, craftsmen were somewhat above the norm, and lower white-collar workers were significantly below the norm. The strong relationship between income and strenuousness of work thus transcends the occupational categories and indicates that within each category those who have more strenuous jobs are more highly rewarded. These data on working addicts thus illustrate one theory of wages (a deviant one at that); wages based on how hard the work is rather than on the level of skill or talent involved.

Strenuousness of work is related to some of the social characteristics of the addicts, but job satisfaction is not. Thus the better educated are less likely to engage in strenuous work than the poorly educated, the Jews less so than the Protestants and Catholics, men more so than women, and Puerto Ricans more so than blacks or whites. The latter finding is somewhat surprising for, as we have seen, the Puerto Ricans are not nearly as well paid as the whites. These data appear in Table 3.12.

As can be seen from reading down the first column, strenuousness of work is related to each of these four social characteristics. Men are almost four times as likely as women to engage in strenuous work; the poorly educated do so much more than the well educated, Protestants much more so than Jews, and Puerto Ricans have more strenuous jobs on the average than blacks and whites. These patterns are somewhat surprising in light of the strong connection between income and strenuous work. Only the sex finding is in keeping with the income data, for the men earn much more on the average than women. But the poorly educated do not earn as much money as the well edu-

Table 3.12

Strenuousness of Work and Job Satisfaction by Sex,
Education, Religion, and Ethnicity

	High strenuousness of work		High on job satisfaction	
	%	N	%	N
Sex				
Male	45	(411)	48	(409)
Female	12	(142)	42	(142)
Education				
Less than high school	52	(292)	45	(292)
High school graduate	36	(154)	45	(154)
Some college	31	(109)	52	(109)
Religion				
Protestant	43	(174)	39	(174)
Catholic	36	(316)	51	(316)
Jew	30	(34)	44	(34)
Ethnicity				
White	45	(228)	50	(228)
Black	39	(220)	40	(220)
Puerto Rican	51	(98)	51	(98)

cated in spite of their greater involvement in strenuous work;
Jews earn much more than Protestants and Catholics, and whites
earn much more than blacks and Puerto Ricans, even though both
Jews and whites score relatively low on strenuous work. These
traits are not as strongly related to job satisfaction. The men
are slightly more likely to be satisfied with their jobs than wom-
en, the well educated somewhat more satisfied than the poorly
educated, Catholics somewhat more satisfied than either Protestants or Jews, and whites and Puerto Ricans are satisfied with
their jobs more often than blacks. That these patterns were
not sharper is somewhat surprising, since each of these traits
is related to income, which we have seen is strongly related
to job satisfaction.

We may conclude this discussion of the characteristics of the jobs that the addicts held by noting that even though many addicts worked in relatively low skilled jobs, the overall level of job satisfaction was rather high. Almost half the addicts were in the high satisfaction category, and only a third in the low category. These working addicts tended to be involved with their jobs, and their drug habit did not diminish their satisfaction with their work. Almost half these addicts had strenuous jobs, but they were amply rewarded for this hard work with higher pay.

As we have seen in this chapter, the occupations of the working addicts were not too different from those of the general population, their earnings compared favorably with the general population, and their jobs were satisfying to many. Addiction to drugs clearly did not force these addicts into the lowest, most poorly paid sectors of the occupational structure. How the various facets of their drug habit that we have enumerated relate to their labor force participation is considered in the next chapter.

4

Labor Force Participation and the Drug Habit

We have seen that there is considerable variation among these addicts in their labor force participation, the types of jobs they held, the industries in which they worked, the length of time they were able to hold their job, the amount they earned, the difficulty of their jobs, and their satisfaction with their jobs. Are these varying outcomes influenced by the addict's drug habit? And do these job characteristics have any influence on the degree to which the addicts became involved with drugs? For example, what effect does age of addiction have on the kinds of jobs the addicts were able to get, and how is strength of habit, as measured by daily cost of drugs, related to labor force participation? And do certain job characteristics, like strenuous work, lead to greater involvement with drugs? These questions are dealt with in this chapter.

Age of Addiction

One might suppose that those who became addicted at an early age were more handicapped than those who became addicts much later in finding good jobs and earning a decent living. The evidence suggests that early addiction was somewhat of a handicap, but not nearly as much as might have been expected. Thus those who became addicted in their early teens were not nearly as likely to have higher white-collar jobs, they were somewhat more likely to be lower white-collar workers, they were more likely to be employed in retailing and less likely to be in other white-collar industries than those who became addicted later, and they were virtually excluded from government employment. The early addicts were more likely than the others to be in the lowest income category (under $100 per week), but they were by no means excluded from the highest income category; in fact, they were as likely to have high earnings as those who became addicted at later ages. Finally, the early addicts were much less likely than the later addicts to hold on to their jobs for relatively long periods of time. These findings are shown in Table 4.1. Rather than present all the categories for each job variable, we present in the table only those categories in which there are patterned differences according to age of addiction.

Table 4.1

Age of Addiction and Aspects of Labor Force Participation
(in %)

	Age of addiction			
	10-16	17-18	19-21	22 plus
Occupation				
Higher white collar	8	3	6	21
Lower white collar	29	38	32	21
Craftsmen	31	29	21	18
Industry				
Retailing	22	19	14	8
Other white collar	19	22	27	33
Government	2	6	8	11
Income				
Under $100	28	19	17	10
$100-199	52	55	68	67
$200 and over	20	20	15	23
Length of employment				
Under 1 year	36	33	29	20
3 or more years	28	22	32	47
N =	(133)	(175)	(147)	(91)

As can be seen from the top row, those in the latest group of addiction, i.e., 22 or older, were much more likely to have higher white-collar jobs than those who got addicted at earlier ages; but significantly, those who got addicted at the earliest age, i.e., under 17, did no worse than those in the two middle groups in getting these more prestigious jobs. Even more strange is the finding that those addicted at an earlier age were more likely than those who became addicted later to get jobs in the relatively prestigious and high-paying category of craftsmen. Thus the proportion of craftsmen steadily declines as age of addiction increases. As for industry, the early addicts tend to be attracted to retailing, the later addicts to other white-collar industries, and hardly any of the earliest addicts end up in government employment. As for income, the early addicts are more prevalent in the lowest category; but perhaps because they are relatively successful in getting high paying craftsmen jobs, they are in the highest income category just as frequently as those who became addicted at older ages.

The strongest relationship is found between age of addiction and length of longest job. The early addicts were not nearly as likely as the older addicts to keep their jobs for three or more years, and they were much more likely to keep them for less than one year. This finding is partially explained by current age, since older addicts, as we have seen, were much more likely to hold the same job for longer periods of time than younger addicts, and younger addicts were more likely to be addicted at a younger age. But even when current age is taken into account, age of addiction is still related to length of employment. Among those currently 25 or less, only 30% of the early addicts held the same job for two years or more, compared with 44% of the addicts who did not get addicted until they were older. Among addicts currently over 25, 50% of the early addicts held jobs for two years or more, and 56% of the late addicts did so — a much smaller gap, but still one suggesting that early addiction is a handicap to lengthy employment. As we have seen, early addiction is one component of involvement with drugs, and thus the more general finding is probably that the greater the drug involvement, the more difficult it is to hold on to a job. We shall consider other evidence bearing on this hypothesis later.

Addiction Relative to First Job

Whether one turned to drugs before entering the labor market
or after, like age of addiction, might be expected to have an impact on the kind of job the addict was able to get and his earnings. This dimension of the drug habit is associated with occupation, industry, and income, as shown in Table 4.2.

Table 4.2

Addiction Relative to Work by Occupation, Industry,
and Income (in %)

	Addicted before first job	Addicted same time	Addicted after first job	N
Occupation				
Higher white collar	16	4	80	(45)
Lower white collar	20	22	58	(174)
Craftsmen	25	10	66	(61)
Semiskilled	22	15	63	(147)
Unskilled	31	12	57	(341)
Industry				
Retailing	24	19	57	(90)
Other white collar	17	15	68	(133)
Manufacturing	27	17	56	(85)
Other blue collar	28	13	59	(204)
Government	9	17	74	(34)
Income (weekly salary)				
Under $100	26	24	50	(105)
$100-149	23	15	62	(220)
$150-199	20	16	64	(122)
$200 and over	23	7	70	(106)

By reading down the first column of Table 4.2 for the occupation data, we see that higher white-collar workers were not

nearly as likely to turn to drugs before work as the unskilled workers. Conversely, from the third column we learn that the great majority (80%) of the higher white-collar workers became addicts only after they entered the labor force, whereas the two relatively low skilled groups — the lower white-collar and the unskilled blue-collar group of laborers and low-level service workers — were least likely to turn to drugs after entering the labor market. Thus when these addicts acquired their habit would seem to have some bearing on the occupations they obtained.

The data for industry shows that retailing, manufacturing, and other blue-collar industries have similar patterns. Roughly a quarter of the workers in these industries became addicts before they went to work, about a fifth became addicts at the same time they entered the labor market, and about three fifths became addicts after they went to work. But other white-collar industries and government show different patterns. In both of these industries those who became addicted before going to work are underrepresented, especially for government, and those who became addicts only after having worked are overrepresented; again, this is particularly true of government. Apparently, government does a better job than other industries of screening out those already addicted at time of employment.

The income patterns are also of some interest. Becoming an addict before entering the labor force apparently is not a deterrent to high earnings, for just as many addicts earning over $200 a week were early addicts as addicts who earned less (the first column in the third part of the table). But the last column of the income data shows that becoming addicted only after entering the labor force is related to income. Thus of those who earned under $100 a week, only half became addicted after going to work. This figure steadily rises with income, reaching 70% of those earning over $200 a week. Thus delaying addiction until after one is established in the labor force does have a payoff with regard to income.

Cost of Drug Habit

The next component of the addict's drug behavior, the cost of his habit, rather than influencing his participation in the world of work, is more likely to be a consequence of it. As noted in the previous chapter, some 24% of the working addicts reported spending less than $20 daily on their habit, 47% spent between $20 and $49, and 29% spent $50 or more daily on drugs. It turns out that the amount spent on drugs varies with occupational group, industrial group, and not surprisingly, income. These findings are shown in Table 4.3.

Table 4.3

Cost of Habit by Occupation, Industry, and Income
(in %)

| | Cost of Habit | | | |
	Under $20	$20-$49	$50 plus	N
Occupation				
Higher white collar	25	36	39	(44)
Lower white collar	30	45	25	(171)
Craftsmen	27	50	23	(60)
Operatives and kindred	23	44	34	(146)
Lower service and laborers	16	57	27	(122)
Industry				
Retailing	21	42	37	(89)
Other white collar	27	47	26	(131)
Manufacturing	33	49	18	(84)
Other blue collar	21	47	33	(200)
Government	15	61	24	(33)
Income (weekly salary)				
Under $100	31	48	20	(103)
$100-149	24	48	28	(215)
$150-199	26	43	31	(121)
$200-249	10	63	27	(48)
$250 and over	21	36	43	(56)

Like the previous tables, the precentages in Table 4.3 add to
100 across each row, and the findings emerge by reading down
the columns. Those in higher white-collar and blue-collar,
other than manufacturing, occupations are more likely than
those in the other occupations to spend a great deal (over $50
daily) on drugs (39% and 34%, respectively). Retailing and blue-
collar industries other than manufacturing lead the other industries with respect to heavy drug users, as measured by cost.
Finally, income is positively related to expenditures for drugs.
With one exception (those in the second highest income group)
the percent spending $50 or more each day on drugs steadily
increases as income increases (the third column in the third
part of the table). This finding suggests that the amount spent
on drugs, or the strength of an addict's habit, is a function of
financial resources. The more money he has to spend, the more
money he will spend on drugs. As we shall see in a later chapter, almost all of these addicts resorted to crime to supplement
their income in supporting their habit. But if crime were the
sole source or primary source of funds for drugs, we should
find no relationship between income and cost of habit. That this
relationship is found indicates that working addicts made use of
their income and not just crime to support their habit.

Number of Drugs and Use of Drugs on Job

The remaining two indicators of involvement with drugs, the
number of illegal hard drugs used and the use of drugs during
the working day, prove to be unrelated to all the job characteristics except one. They are not related to occupation, industry,
length of longest job, number of jobs, strenuousness of work, or
job satisfaction. (These last two variables prove to be unrelated
to any of the drug involvement dimensions.) The exception is
income. Just as income was strongly related to the amount
spent on drugs each day, so it is strongly related to the number
of drugs used and the use of drugs during the working day, as
can be seen from Table 4.4.

The findings in Table 4.4, coupled with the earlier finding on

Table 4.4

Income (Weekly Wages) by Number of Drugs Used and
Use of Drugs during Working Day (in %)

	Under $100	$100-149	$150-199	$200-249	$250+
Number of drugs 3 or more	17	17	25	26	30
Used drugs during workday	69	83	88	86	93

the strong relationship between income and cost of habit,
strongly suggest that the degree to which addicts become involved with drugs is largely dependent on their resources. If
they can afford it, they will use a lot of drugs both in terms of
quantity and quality, and they will indulge their drug habit during the working day. Since income is related to better-quality
jobs and length of employment, it can be taken as a measure of
success in the occupational world. In this context these findings
seem to mean that the more successful the addict was in the occupational world, the more heavily involved he became with
drugs. Conversely, a heavy drug habit was apparently not a
handicap to occupational success as measured by income.

Drug Involvement Index

    As noted in the previous chapter, we have constructed an in-
dex of drug involvement based on number of drugs, cost of
drugs, and use of drugs during the working day. This index is
not related to occupation, industry, number of jobs, or length
of longest job. But just as each of its components was related
to income, so is the aggregate index. The only new discovery
is that drug involvement as measured by this index is related
to strenuousness of work. These findings appear in Table 4.5.
    From the third column of the income part of the table, it can
be seen that high involvement steadily increases with income,
as was found in Table 4.4. That strenuousness of work is also

Table 4.5

Drug Involvement by Income and Strenuousness
of Work Index (in %)

	Low	Medium	High	N
Income (weekly salary)				
Under $100	29	54	17	(104)
$100-149	15	69	16	(220)
$150-199	11	64	25	(122)
$200-249	14	60	26	(50)
$250 plus	5	64	31	(56)
Strenuousness of work				
Low	16	68	16	(224)
Medium low	16	64	20	(88)
Medium high	19	57	24	(101)
High	13	60	27	(141)

related positively to drug involvement is highly suggestive.
This could be an artifact of the more strenuous jobs being on
the average better paying than the less strenuous ones; but even
when income is taken into account there is still some association
between strenuousness of work and drug involvement, as can be
seen from Table 4.6.

Table 4.6

High Drug Involvement Index by Strenuousness
of Work and Income

	Strenuousness of work			
	Low		High	
Weekly income	%	N	%	N
Under $150	31	(193)	41	(120)
$150-199	42	(65)	48	(52)
$200 and over	52	(42)	57	(60)

The columns of Table 4.6 show that income is related to drug involvement among both those with strenuous and nonstrenuous jobs, but of more interest are the patterns shown by the rows of the table. On each income level those with the more strenuous jobs are more likely to be highly involved in drugs. This strongly suggests that strenuous work is an inducement to becoming involved with drugs. Conversations with former employees in the construction industry revealed that many construction workers use drugs at work to relieve the pain stemming from their physically difficult jobs. It is conceivable, then, that people whose jobs are strenuous in that they involve hard physical labor or are dirty and dangerous use drugs to help them adapt to their working conditions.

This suggestive finding brings to a close our examination of how various aspects of labor force participation and job characteristics relate to drug use.

5

The Impact of Drugs on the Job

The working addicts, especially those who reported that they used drugs at work, were asked a number of questions about their drug habit in the work setting, ranging from the number of times they took drugs during the working day, to their reasons for taking drugs at work, to the impact of drugs on their work performance. These issues are dealt with in this chapter.

As we saw in Chapter 2, fully 82% of the sample said that they did take drugs during the working day. Of this group, 41% took drugs only once during the workday, 34% took drugs twice, and 25% took drugs three or more times while at work. How frequently drugs were taken at work is related to a number of characteristics of the addicts. Thus men were more likely than women to take drugs more than once a day at work (55% compared with 37%), Jews more so than either Protestants or Catholics (71% compared with 51 and 50%), and whites more so than blacks or Puerto Ricans (60% compared with 44 and 43%). Of particular significance, income turns out to be strongly related to how often drugs are taken during the workday. Of those who used drugs at work, only 35% of the poorest paid, those earning under $100 a week, used drugs two or more times; among those earning $100-149, this figure rises to 48%, and it climbs to 58% for those earning between $150 and $199 and between $200 and $249; in the highest income group, those over $250 a week, multiple use during the workday soars to 66%. From this finding it would seem that the frequency of drug use

64

during the workday is as much dependent on the addict's resources as on his need.

When asked their reason for taking drugs on the job, 43% re-
plied that they took drugs to avoid sickness, 17% said they took
drugs to feel good or get high, and 40% said they took drugs for
both reasons. These reasons are pretty much unrelated to the
social characteristics of the addicts, with the exception that
women were more often motivated to avoid illness only than
were men who had an interest in getting high as well. Also, the
oldest addicts, those over 30, took drugs primarily to avoid illness (57%), whereas a majority of younger addicts were inter-
ested in feeling good as well.

Apart from their reason for taking drugs, the respondents
were asked whether the drugs they took at work did in fact make
them high, and the great majority, 72%, said that they did experience this effect. Getting high from drugs at work turns out to
be very much a youth phenomenon. The younger addicts were
much more likely to answer in the affirmative than older addicts, although in every age group a majority admitted that taking drugs made them high. Thus among those between 17 and
21, 89% said the drugs made them high, 81% of the 22-24 year
olds, 70% of the 25-29 year olds, and only 60% of the addicts
30 and over. Not surprisingly, men were more likely to get
high from drugs on the job than women, 75% compared with 64%.
Other characteristics, such as education, ethnicity, and religion,
are not related to this issue. When the percent who got high
from drugs at work is calculated on the basis of the total sample, including those who did not take drugs at work, we find that
54% fall into this category. In short, a majority of addicts who
held jobs experienced the sensations of the "high" while at work.

Given the fact that most addicts got high during the workday,
what effect did this have on their work? When asked whether
taking drugs made their work harder, easier, or had no effect
on their work, 14% said that it made their work harder, 27%
said it had no effect on their work, but a majority, 59% said
that it made their work easier. This feeling that drugs made
their jobs easier provides an important clue to why these addicts

used drugs at work. We might suppose that those employed in
highly strenuous jobs would be much more likely to say that
drugs made their jobs easier, but in fact there is only a very
weak relationship between the strenuousness of work index and
this response. Thus of those who score low on strenuous work,
55% said that drugs made their jobs easier, compared with 62%
of those in the medium category and 61% of those in the high
group. Similarly, those in blue-collar employment were only
slightly more likely to give this response than those in white-
collar work (63% for craftsmen, 62% for the semiskilled, and
60% of the unskilled, compared with 53% of the higher white
collar and 55% of the lower white collar). But how drugs affected the addict's work is very much related to age. Older
addicts were more likely than younger addicts to say that they
made their jobs easier. These responses are in keeping with
the earlier finding that older addicts took drugs at work to avoid
sickness and younger addicts for the thrills. This finding is
shown in Table 5.1.

Table 5.1

Impact of Drugs on Work by Age
(in %)

Impact on work	17-21	22-24	25-29	30 plus
Harder	10	13	13	21
Easier	67	59	59	53
No effect	23	28	28	27

The impact of drugs on work is not related to sex or to race.
Women were just as likely as men to say that drugs made their
work harder or easier, and the responses of whites, blacks, and
Puerto Ricans were quite similar. Oddly enough, religion does
make a difference. We have seen that Jews were much more
likely than Protestants or Catholics to take drugs more than
once during the working day. Either because of, or in spite of,
this heavy drug use, Jews were more likely than either Protes-

tants or Catholics to say that drugs made their work harder —
21% compared with 13 and 11%. The responses of the various
occupational groups were quite similar, with one exception:
craftsmen were much less likely than those in other occupations
to say that drugs made their work harder (only 6% compared
with 12 to 17% of the other occupations) and more likely to say
that drugs made their work easier (63% compared to 53 to 62%
[semiskilled] of the other occupations). Neither industry nor
income shows any consistent relationships to the impact of drugs
on work, and both job satisfaction and strenuousness of work
are unrelated to this variable.

The respondents were asked about two other potential consequences of drug use for their work life: whether they fell asleep
on the job because of drugs, and whether they missed days of
work because of their drug habit. Almost a third of the addicts
(31%) said that they had fallen asleep at work because of drugs
(usually in the restroom), and more than half (53%) said that
their drug habit had caused them to miss days of work. Falling
asleep on the job is not related to age, education, or income.
Men were somewhat more likely to say yes to this question than
women (33% versus 25%), and whites more so than blacks or
Puerto Ricans (35% compared with 27 and 25%). Craftsmen reported falling asleep most often (38%) and higher white-collar
workers least often (22%); and those who worked for government
fell asleep most often (39%), whereas those who worked for retailing establishments fell asleep least often (27%).

Missing days from work because of drugs turns out to be more
characteristic of men, the well educated, and the Jews. The
figures for men and women are 57 and 44%, for poorly educated
50%, well educated 60%, and for Jews 65%, compared with 58%
for Catholics and 46% for Protestants. Whites missed work because of drugs more often than blacks and Puerto Ricans (62%
compared with 43 and 53%). Craftsmen had the highest absentee-
ism rate of any occupational group (61%), and semiskilled
workers had the lowest rate (48%); as for industry, government
employees had the highest rate (61%), and retail employees the
lowest (49%).

The various consequences of drug use for the job tend to be related to each other. For example, those who fell asleep on the job were much more likely to get high from drugs at work; they were much more likely to take drugs to feel good and not simply to avoid sickness; they were much more likely to take drugs at least twice during the working day; they were more likely to report that drugs affected their work in some way; and they were more likely to have missed work because of drugs. Similarly large differences apply to the associations between other consequences of taking drugs. These associations are shown in Table 5.2.

Table 5.2 shows that some of these dimensions of drug use on the job yield higher correlations than others. Getting high from drugs at work (item 3) and falling asleep on the job (item 5) are closely associated with almost all the other dimensions. Other characteristics relate to some but not all the traits, such as reasons for taking the drugs (item 2) and the effect that taking drugs had on one's work (item 4). One of these dimensions has only weak relationships, if any, to the others, and that is the number of times drugs are taken during the working day (item 1). We have seen that this attribute is closely linked to income, but it only seems to affect the likelihood that the person would fall asleep on the job (as the data show a moderate relationship between frequency and this trait). Since the other five items shown in Table 5.2 are reasonably well related to each other, we have combined them into an index of the impact of drugs on the addict's job. In developing this index, we have assigned a score of 1 to each of the following responses: (a) taking drugs to feel good or to feel good and avoid illness, (b) getting high at work, (c) reporting that drugs make work harder or easier, (d) falling asleep at work because of drugs, and (e) missing work because of drugs. The resulting index has been split into three categories: low impact, consisting of 30% of the cases including those who did not use drugs as work; medium impact, consisting of 42%; and high impact, consisting of 28%.

Surprisingly, the index of the impact of drugs on the job is not related to age, as the relatively young and old addicts report

Table 5.2

The Associations between Various Aspects of Drug Taking
on the Job (in %)

	1. Number of times drugs taken			2. Reasons for taking drugs		
				Avoid illness	Feel good	Both
	One	Two	Three			
1. 2 or more times	—	—	—	49	65	64
2. Avoid illness	52	35	40	—	—	—
3. Get high	64	77	81	47	89	96
4. No effect	26	26	29	27	24	29
5. Fall asleep	22	37	38	22	31	41
6. Miss work	57	56	55	53	48	64

	3. Get high at work		4. Drugs make work		
	Yes	No	Harder	Easier	No effect
1. 2 or more times	63	44	65	56	59
2. Avoid illness	29	87	36	45	43
3. Get high	—	—	82	71	70
4. No effect	26	29	—	—	—
5. Fall asleep	35	15	53	31	19
6. Miss work	60	42	74	58	44

	5. Fall asleep on job		6. Miss days of work	
	Yes	No	Yes	No
1. 2 or more times	70	52	58	60
2. Avoid illness	31	49	40	47
3. Get high	86	66	60	40
4. No effect	17	31	21	35
5. Fall asleep	—	—	41	18
6. Miss work	75	48	—	—

similar proportions of low and high impact. But the index is related to some other social characteristics, notably sex, education,
religion, and ethnicity. These findings are shown in Table 5.3.

Table 5.3

Impact of Drugs on Job by Sex, Education,
Religion, and Ethnicity (in %)

Impact of	Sex		Education		
drugs on job	Men	Women	Low	Medium	High
Low	26	40	34	27	21
Medium	42	40	40	42	45
High	32	20	26	31	34
N =	(413)	(142)	(292)	(154)	(109)

	Religion			Ethnicity		
Impact of drugs on job	Prot.	Cath.	Jew	White	Black	Puerto Rican
Low	41	26	21	20	37	37
Medium	37	40	56	45	42	36
High	22	34	24	35	21	28
N =	(174)	(316)	(34)	(228)	(220)	(98)

Men are more likely than women to say that drugs had an impact on their work, the better educated show a higher impact than the poorly educated, the Protestants were less likely than Catholics or Jews to report that drugs affected their work life. Jews appear in the low category much less often than Protestants, but they are concentrated in the medium category, with the result that Catholics show the highest proportion in the high impact group. Finally, whites were much more likely to have drugs affect their work life than blacks, with Puerto Ricans in between.

When the impact of drugs on the job index is related to the various work variables examined in Chapter 3, few relationships emerge. Contrary to what was expected, it is not related to strenuousness of work, to job satisfaction, or to industry. Craftsmen score higher on the index than those in the other occupational groups, and those of higher income tend to score higher than those of lower income. The latter relationships are shown in Table 5.4.

Table 5.4

Index of Drug Impact on Job by Occupation and Income
(in %)

	Low	Medium	High	N
Occupation				
Higher white collar	29	47	24	(45)
Lower white collar	32	42	26	(174)
Craftsmen	36	28	36	(61)
Semiskilled	26	47	27	(147)
Unskilled	27	42	31	(125)
Income (weekly salary)				
Under $100	46	34	20	(105)
$100-149	30	41	29	(220)
$150-199	22	45	33	(122)
$200-249	32	36	32	(50)
$250 and over	13	55	32	(56)

The various occupational groupings are quite similar with respect to the impact of drugs on their jobs, with the exception of
craftsmen. The craftsmen turn out to be doubly deviant. They
not only have the largest proportion in the high-impact group,
but they also have the largest proportion in the low-impact
group. On this basis it would seem that there is hardly anything
about the work that craftsmen do that would force them into one
or another category on this variable.

Reading down the first column of the income part of the table,
we find that with one exception, low impact on job steadily declines as income increases. Those who earned under $100 a
week are more than three times as likely to be in the low-impact
category as those in the highest income category. The exception
to this pattern is found in the second highest income group,
where the percent in the low category increases. At the other
extreme of high impact, those who earned less than $100 a week
were well below those who earned more. We have seen that income was related to the frequency of taking drugs at work, and
we now see that it is related to the general index of the impact

of drugs on jobs. The same interpretation seems appropriate. Those who earn more can afford to buy more drugs, they use more drugs per day, with the result that their habit had a measurable impact on their work routine.

Not surprisingly, the degree to which the addict's habit affected his workday is strongly related to the degree to which he was involved with drugs. Those who were most involved in drugs as measured by the amount of money they spent on drugs, the number of drugs they used, and their reliance on drugs at work were most likely to report a high impact of drugs on their job, as can be seen from Table 5.5.

Table 5.5

The Impact of Drugs on the Job by Drug Involvement (in %)

Impact of drugs on job	Drug involvement		
	Low	Medium	High
Low	82	25	19
Medium	13	48	44
High	6	27	37
N =	(71)	(244)	(217)

From the top row we see low impact on job shrinks dramatically as drug involvement increases, from a high of 82% to a low of 19%. The relationship is also evident at the other extreme, if not so pronounced.

Apart from the impact of drugs on the addict's feeling states and performance while at work, the respondents were asked whether their use of drugs at work resulted in any accidents to themselves, other people, or equipment. Such injury and damage resulting from drugs proved to be relatively rare. When asked whether they ever injured themselves while on the job, 100 persons in the sample, 18% in all, answered affirmatively. But when asked whether this injury had anything to do with their drug use, only 28 persons, 5% of the sample and 28% of the injured, said yes. Although this number is relatively small compared with the number injured, it is nonetheless true that the rate of personal injuries in this group increased by 39% as a result of their drug use (calculated on the basis of the number of injuries not drug related divided into the number of drug-related injuries). From the viewpoint of the insurance programs concerned with industrial accidents, this is by no means an insignificant figure.

When asked whether they had ever caused any damage to equipment while at work, 78 persons said they had, a figure that amounts to 14% of the sample. Damage to equipment was much more likely than personal injury to be drug related, for 38 persons in this group said that their use of drugs led to the damage of equipment, or 49% of all the cases of equipment damage. This amounts to a whopping 95% increase in the rate of equipment damage among these workers due to drugs. These rates apply, of course, only to working addicts and cannot be generalized to the entire work force.

Finally, when asked whether they had ever caused any other person at work to be injured, 24 persons, a mere 4% of the entire sample, answered affirmatively. Of this group, 6 persons said that this accident stemmed from their use of drugs, a figure amounting to 25% of the group that had caused such injuries to others. Drugs increased this rate of hurting others while at work by 33%. Some of the people in the sample were involved in more than one of these drug-related accidents. In all, 57 persons, or 10% of the sample, were responsible for at least one of these types of accidents.

When the index of drug-related accidents is related to the respondents' social characteristics, several relationships emerge. The very young, those between 17 and 21, were more likely to be involved in such accidents than older addicts, 16% compared with 8 to 11% of the groups of older addicts. Men were more than twice as likely to have had such accidents as women, 12% compared with 5%; Jews more than Catholics and Protestants, 18% compared with 10% and 5% (the Jewish rate is more than three times as high as the Protestant rate); and whites were twice as likely to have such accidents as blacks and Puerto Ricans, 14% compared with 8% and 7%.

Craftsmen, whom we have seen were most likely to have drugs
affect their work roles, were also most likely of any occupational group to be involved in these drug-related accidents, 16%.
They are closely followed by the semiskilled, who have 14% in
this group. Higher white-collar workers were least likely to
be involved in drug-related accidents, as only 2% of them had
this experience. Addicts who had been employed in retailing
were most accident prone because of drugs, 16%, while those
who worked in other white-collar industries or government
were least prone to these accidents, 5 and 6%, respectively.
We saw in an earlier chapter that involvement with drugs steadily increased with income, and as we shall soon see, drug involvement is very much related to accidents stemming from
the use of drugs. For this reason, perhaps, income shows a
marked relationship to drug-related accidents. As income increases, so does the rate of such accidents, until the highest
income group is reached, when suddenly the accident rate falls
sharply. Thus among those earning under $100 a week, only
7% had drug-related accidents. This figure climbs to 11% in
the next highest income group ($100-149), to 12% in the next highest,
reaching 18% in the group earning between $200 and $249 a week.
But then among the relatively small number earning over $250
a week, the rate drops precipitously to 5%. Having such accidents is not related to job satisfaction, but it is related to how
strenuous the work is. Among those who score low on strenuousness of work, the accident rate is 6%, and for those in the
medium catetory it is 5%; but among those who score high on
this index, the rate shoots up to 16%. This is most likely explained on the grounds that accidents, whether drug caused or
not, are likely to increase sharply in the jobs that involve strenuous work.

Not surprisingly, the more involved in drugs the addict was,
and the more drugs affected his work routine, the more likely
he was to be involved in drug-related accidents to himself,
others, and equipment. These findings are shown in Table 5.6.

As drug involvement increases and as the impact of drugs on
the job increases, so does the rate of drug-related accidents.

Table 5.6

Drug-Related Accidents by Drug Involvement Index
and Impact of Drugs on Job Index
(in %)

	Drug involvement			Impact of drugs on job	
	%	N		%	N
Low	1	(71)	Low	4	(165)
Medium	7	(244)	Medium	9	(231)
High	16	(217)	High	20	(159)

In both instances the shift from medium to high on the indexes
results in a very sharp increase in accidents. Table 5.6 clearly
demonstrates that excessive drug involvement in general and
more specifically at work tends to be costly for the addict, his
co-workers, and his employer. By the same token, most addicts
manage to avoid drug-related accidents; and if addicts use drugs
only in moderation both in general and at the work place, they
run little risk of serious accidents.

To close out this analysis of the impact of drugs on the addict's job, we consider data bearing on how well these addicts
performed their jobs. People may or may not be good judges of
their role performances, and addicts in particular may be prone
to distortion in their self-perceptions. Other research has
shown that people tend to exaggerate their performances in a
wide range of areas. For example, when students are asked
whether they fall into the top quarter, second quarter, third
quarter, or bottom quarter of their class, their judgments do
not distribute evenly in the four quarters. Very few students
perceive themselves as being in the bottom quarter, and the majority place themselves in the first or second quarter. For this
reason, we might look with some suspicion at how these addicts
rated themselves in terms of how well they performed their jobs.
Nevertheless, the patterns of relationship involving these ratings
are of considerable interest even if the absolute percentages
are suspect. The addicts were asked two questions relating to
the issue of how well they did their job: first, how good a job

did their supervisors think they were doing, and second, how
good a job did they think they were doing. To both questions a
substantial majority gave themselves the highest rating; but
significantly, they were more critical of themselves than they
thought their supervisors were. These data are shown in Table
5.7.

Table 5.7

Rating of Job Performance by Supervisors and Self
(in %)

	Supervisor's rating	Self rating
Very good	64	62
Fairly good	32	29
Not too good	4	9
N =	(555)	(555)

Fully 64% of the working addicts believed that their supervisors thought they were doing a very good job, and almost as
many, 62%, gave themselves this high rating. About a third felt
that their supervisors would rate their performance as fairly
good, and only a tiny fraction, 4%, felt that they would receive
a bad rating from their supervisors. The working addicts tended
to be somewhat tougher on themselves. More than twice as
many, 9%, rated their performance as "not too good." That almost all of the addicts thought their boss considered them doing
a fairly good or very good job and that almost as many gave
themselves such high ratings strongly suggests that addiction
is not a serious handicap to job performance. Even if these addicts do tend to exaggerate how well they did their job, it is evident that most of them were not presented with clear evidence
that they were failing at their work. This finding is in keeping
with the earlier finding that many addicts kept their jobs for a
fairly long period of time. Contrary to the popular stereotype
of the debilitating consequences of addiction, most working addicts were able to integrate their work life with their drug habit
fairly well and were able to perform their jobs rather well in the
process.

That addicts may be fairly accurate in how they perceive their job performances finds some confirmation in the fact that their assessments of how well they performed are not related to their social characteristics. Were these evaluations highly subjective, with little basis in reality, then social characteristics might be expected to influence their perceptions; but this is not the case. Thus evaluations of job performance by supervisors and self are not related to age, sex, education, or religion, and the supervisors' evaluation is not related to ethnicity as well. Inexplicably, self-evaluation of performance does vary with ethnicity, with blacks giving themselves a below average evaluation (only 57% judge their performance as very good), and Puerto Ricans an above average evaluation (70% very good). But with this one exception, the social characteristics of the addicts are not related to their assessments of their job performance.

In contrast to social characteristics, a number of the work variables are related to assessments of job performance. Craftsmen are most likely to rate their job performances as high, followed by the semiskilled operators, transport workers, and maintenance men. Both higher and lower white-collar workers and unskilled workers (the laborers and lower-level service workers) rate their job performances lower. Government workers are more harsh on their job performances than workers in other industries, and better paid workers, not surprisingly, tend to rate their job performances higher than poorer paid workers. These relationships are shown in Tables 5.8 and 5.9

From the top part of the table we see that craftsmen are most likely to perceive their supervisors as giving them a very good rating, and they are even more likely to assign this high rating to themselves (70 and 74%). Lower white-collar workers and unskilled are most harsh on themselves, assigning a lower rating to themselves than they think their supervisors would. The bottom half of the table shows that government workers are least likely to think their bosses would rate them highly, and they concur by also rating themselves as performing less than very well

more often than any other group. Little variation is found among
the other industries.

Table 5.8

Percent Reporting Very Good Job Performance as Judged
by Superiors and Self by Occupation and Industry

	Occupation				
	Higher white collar	Lower white collar	Craftsmen	Semi-skilled	Unskilled
Supervisors	59	66	70	66	60
Self	60	58	74	67	58

	Industry				
	Retailing	Other white collar	Manufacturing	Other blue collar	Government
Supervisors	68	67	66	61	56
Self	66	63	69	57	53

The impact of income and job satisfaction on assessments of
job performance are shown in Table 5.9.

Table 5.9

Percent Reporting Very Good Job Performance as Judged
by Supervisors and Self by Income and Job Satisfaction

	Income				
	$40-99	$100-149	$150-199	$200-249	$250 and over
Supervisors	49	63	74	76	67
Self	50	60	71	64	70

	Job satisfaction		
	Low	Medium	High
Supervisors	49	65	76
Self	50	65	70

From the income part of the table we see that as income increases so do assessments of job performance. Perceptions of evaluations by supervisors steadily increase until the highest income group is reached, where they fall somewhat. Self assessments also tend to go up with income, with a fall-off in the group earning between $200 and $249 a week. For some inexplicable reason, the people in this income group are much tougher on themselves than they think their supervisors are. Thus 76% of this income group think their supervisors give them a good rating, the highest figure of any income group, but only 64% of this group rate themselves as very good, a discrepancy of 12 percentage points. The tendency of perceived job performance to be related to income is not surprising for, after all, income is to some extent a reward for doing one's job well.

The strongest relationship to perceived job performance is found in the job satisfaction section of Table 5.9. Assessments of job performance increase sharply with job satisfaction. This too is not surprising. The more satisfied people are with their jobs, the more likely they are to perform well. This finding contains an important lesson for management and industry. In order to get workers to perform well in their jobs, it is important to create the conditions in the work place that allow workers to like their jobs. Clearly, job satisfaction and job performance go hand in hand.

Remaining to be considered are the variables relating to drug involvement and drug impact. Surprisingly enough, the degree of involvement in drugs as measured by number of different drugs taken regularly, amount spent on drugs, and reliance on drugs while at work is not related to assessments of job performance. Neither the rating attributed to supervisors nor one's own rating is related to drug involvement. But the impact of drugs on the job index and the drug-related accident index are related to assessments of job performance. These relationships are shown in Table 5.10.

The job index section in Table 5.10 shows that the greater the impact of drugs on the work routine of the respondents, the lower their assessment of their job performance. This holds true to

Table 5.10

Those Reporting Very Good Job Performance as Judged
by Supervisors and Self by Impact of Drugs on Job
and Drug-Related Accidents

	Impact of drugs on job index					
	Low		Medium		High	
	%	N	%	N	%	N
Supervisors	73	(164)	67	(230)	52	(157)
Self	70	(165)	64	(231)	51	(159)

	Drug-related accidents (in %)	
	None	One or more
Supervisors	67	42
Self	63	53

about the same extent for their guess as to how their supervisors would rate them and how they rate themselves. The accident section of Table 5.10 shows a strong relationship between
involvement in drug-related accidents and assessments of how
supervisors would rate their job performance. For the first
time we find a majority claiming that their supervisors did not
think they did a very good job (among those who were involved
in drug-related accidents). Apparently, when an addict's addiction causes a serious mishap at work, he loses face with his
supervisors. The addicts themselves do not consider this as
serious a setback to their job performance, as substantially
more of those involved in accidents give themselves a good rating than think their supervisors would (53% compared with 42%).
As a result, involvement in accidents has a much smaller impact on their own ratings of their job performance than on their
assessment of their supervisors' ratings of them.

This concludes our examination of the impact of the addict's
drug habit on his work life. We have seen that most working
addicts bring their habit to the work place, using illegal drugs
during the workday, for many, to avoid feelings of sickness and,
for many more, to feel high. Most of them do in fact get high

while on the job, but their use of drugs does not interfere drastically with their job performances. Most of them claim that
drugs make their jobs easier, but a minority report that drugs
cause them to fall asleep on the job and that they miss days of
work because of their habit. A fraction of the workers, 10% in
all, report that drugs caused them to have accidents at work;
but these costs notwithstanding, most addicts felt that they performed their jobs very well and that their supervisors gave
them very good job ratings as well. These data develop a picture somewhat at odds with the common stereotype of addict
behavior. The stereotype has it that addicts are more or less
spaced out when under the influence of drugs and can hardly
function in normal ways at all. These data suggest that in spite
of use of drugs on the job and feelings of being high, most working addicts are able to get their job done and meet the expecta-
tions of their supervisors.

So far we have considered the working addict in isolation at
his place of work. But in reality workers have colleagues and
bosses. What is the impact of drugs on the work culture? This
question is addressed in the next chapter.

6

The Drug Culture at the Work Place

Most people carry out their work in some kind of a social setting — a factory, a store, a hospital, a school, an office — in
which they have social relationships with other people, e.g., co-
workers, supervisors, customers, and clients. To what extent
is on-the-job drug use part of a drug culture that has intruded
on the work place? Were the working addicts we interviewed
so discrete that none of their co-workers knew of their drug
habit? If more than one addict worked for the same firm, did
they keep their secret from each other? Or did drugs become
a part of the patterns of sociability at work to the point where
a drug culture might be said to have penetrated the work place?
This chapter deals with this issue. We know whether our respondents knew if any of their co-workers were addicts, whether
their co-workers and bosses knew about their addiction, and
their attitudes toward the addict if they did know. And we know
whether drugs were bought and sold at the work place, and
whether the people we interviewed started to use certain drugs
for the first time at work, that is, whether the work place is
ever the breeding ground for the drug habit. As we shall see
from an examination of this information, drug cultures have indeed emerged at many places of work. Not only is the individ-
ual addict able to work while addicted to drugs, but his habit and
those of his co-workers have generated a drug culture that has
somehow become integrated into the work place.

The Incidence of Drug Users at Work

The respondents were asked several questions about drug use by their co-workers: how many of the people in their section of the firm were addicts and how many of all the employees of the firm were addicts; how many of the people in their section and how many in the whole firm smoked marijuana at work. Unfortunately, these questions failed to differentiate the respondent from the others. Many respondents included themselves when answering, while others interpreted the questions to mean people other than themselves. Thus in some instances the interviewers recorded a "zero" in the response category, meaning no other users, and in other instances the interviewers entered a "one," meaning only the respondent. We have thus treated the response "zero" as identical to the response "one" signifying the respondent as the only addict. This decision undoubtedly means that we have underestimated the instances of other addicts, for in some instances the entry "one" no doubt meant another addict in addition to the respondent. With this caveat in mind, we present in Table 6.1 the frequencies for each of these questions.

Table 6.1

Frequency of Drug Addiction and Marijuana Smoking in
Section and Total Firm (in %)

Frequency	Addicts		Marijuana smokers	
	Section	Firm	Section	Firm
1 (Respondent only)	72	60	52	48
2	12	11	15	6
3	6	7	9	6
4-6	6	10	13	14
7-9	1	3	3	5
10 and over	3	9	8	21
N =	(521)	(440)	(500)	(437)

Before examining the distributions, notice should be taken of the base figures. The respondents were not nearly as likely to have such information about the entire firm as they were about the section in which they worked; hence many fewer answered the questions about the total firm. But even the questions about the sections could not be answered by all the respondents, primarily because some of the respondents had jobs that did not involve working in sections of companies, such as window cleaners, or doormen, or dog walkers. Also, it must be kept in mind that there was considerable variation in the size of the firm for which these addicts worked, with size ranging from 36 persons to over 45,000, with 2,470 as the average firm size. We have not bothered to standardize the frequency questions by taking into account the size of the firm or the size of the section, although some addicts worked in such small sections or firms that not more than a handful of others could have been users, and others worked in such large firms that even ten or more addicts might go largely unnoticed in the crowd. Nonetheless, the absolute frequency distributions shown in Table 6.1 are of considerable interest. In most of the firms the respondent was the only drug addict. This was true of 72% of the work sections and 60% of the firms. By the same token, in 28% of the cases the addict had at least one fellow addict in his work section, and in 40% of the cases the addict knew of at least one other person who was an addict in his firm. Some 12% of the respondents reported that one other person in their section was also an addict, 12% knew of two to six other addicts in their section, and 3% (14 persons) reported that there were ten or more addicts in their section. As expected, the respondents reported substantially more addicts in the total firm than in their own section. In 22% of the cases there were at least three other addicts working for the firm, and in 9% there were ten or more addicts employed by the firm. These are rather startling figures. If the working addicts we interviewed were employed in firms representative of New York City's industries, then more than one out of every five firms employs at least four addicts, and one out of every ten employs at least ten addicts.

Pot smoking turns out to be quite common in the work place.

Almost half of the addicts reported at least one other marijuana smoker besides themselves in their work section, and more than half reported at least one other in the entire firm. A third of the addicts reported at least two other persons besides themselves smoked pot in their work section, and almost half of the addicts worked in firms where at least two others besides themselves smoked marijuana on the job. The national figures on marijuana use show a dramatic increase in users over the past decade or so. We now know that marijuana smoking is so common that more than half of the firms in New York have employees who smoke pot on the job.

These questions about drug users on the job are all related to each other. If the respondent reported addicts in his work section, he was almost sure to report additional addicts in the rest of the company, and the more addicts in the company, the more the number who smoked pot in both the section and the whole firm. But use of hard drugs, particularly heroin, is quite different from smoking pot, which has become rather chic in many circles, and for this reason we shall analyze the prevalence of hard drug users and marijuana smokers separately. The question about users in the section has been combined with the question about users in the company for both hard drugs and for marijuana. And the tables to be presented show the percent who report other addicts and pot smokers at their place of work.

Social characteristics of respondents and drug users at work. The first question to be considered is whether certain kinds of addicts migrate to work settings in which there are other drug users. Is there any connection between the social characteristics of the addicts in our sample and having work colleagues who use drugs? The answer is yes, since a number of social characteristics, such as sex, age, education, and religion, are related to the frequency of drug users at the work place. For example, men are much more likely than women to have work colleagues who are also addicts and who smoke pot. Thus almost half the men, 46%, reported at least one other co-worker was an addict, compared with 29% of the women; and 59% of the men reported that co-workers smoked pot on the job, compared

with 40% of the women. The addicts under 25 were somewhat
more likely than those over 25 to have work associates who
were also addicts and much more likely to have work associates
who smoked pot (Table 6.2).

Table 6.2

Drug Users among Work Associates by Age
(in %)

	17-21	22-24	25-29	30 plus
Addicts among co-workers	47	51	35	40
Pot smokers among co-workers	63	58	51	49

As can be seen from the top row, the age pattern is somewhat
irregular, with the critical distinction between those under 25
and those over 25. About half of the addicts under 25 managed
to find a place of work in which at least one other person was
an addict, whereas only a third of two fifths of the older addicts
had a fellow addict among their work colleagues. Marijuana
smoking in the work place is much more closely associated with
age. As the age of the addict drops, the percent who worked in
settings where pot was smoked steadily increases.

The education of the respondent turns out to be negatively related to having co-workers who are addicts but positively related
to having co-workers who smoke pot, as can be seen from Table
6.3.

Table 6.3

Drug Users among Co-workers by Education
(in %)

	Less than HS grad.	HS grad.	Some college
Addict co-workers	45	43	31
Pot smoking co-workers	52	53	63

The poorly educated are more likely to be employed in firms with other addicts than the well educated, but the reverse is true for the prevalence of pot smoking at work. The better educated are attracted to work settings in which pot smoking is fashionable. This probably reflects the widespread acceptability of pot smoking among the well educated in America. In industries that require well-educated employees, such as the mass media, advertising, publishing, banking, and insurance, the more mildly deviant drug abuse of marijuana smoking is apt to be prevalent.

Religion is another social characteristic linked to the presence of other drug users at work. Protestants are more likely than Catholics to have co-workers who are also addicts, 49% compared with 39%, and Jews are least likely to report co-workers who are addicts, 23%. As for co-workers who are pot smokers, there is no difference between Protestants and Catholics (about 55% of both groups say that pot smoking goes on where they worked), but Jews again were least likely to say that their co-workers engaged in this practice, with 45% answering affirmatively. Ethnicity turns out to be another characteristic yielding quite different patterns for the two drug questions. Blacks were somewhat more likely than whites and Puerto Ricans to report co-workers who were addicts, but they were least likely to report co-workers who smoked pot, as can be seen from Table 6.4.

Table 6.4

Drug Users among Co-workers by Ethnicity
(in %)

	Whites	Blacks	Puerto Ricans
Addict co-workers	38	46	37
Pot smoking co-workers	57	50	53

Whereas blacks are most likely to report other addicts among their co-workers, it is the whites who are most likely to report pot smoking by their colleagues at work, a finding in keeping with the earlier patterns on education.

Job characteristics and drug users at work. Were addicts
employed in certain kinds of occupations and industries more
likely to have co-workers who used drugs? Contrary to what
we might have expected, occupation is not related to having co-
workers who used drugs, with the exception that those employed
in lower white-collar occupations, clerical and sales workers,
were least likely to report addicts or pot smokers among their
co-workers. But the difference was not large in either instance,
and the other occupations were quite similar to each other. But
if occupation is not related to drug use by co-workers, industry
is. Government employees were much more likely to report
fellow addicts among their co-workers than addicts employed
in any other industry, and the government employees also led
in reports of pot smokers among their colleagues. In second
place are those employed in manufacturing, and at the bottom
are those who worked in retailing. These data are shown in
Table 6.5.

Table 6.5

Drug Users among Co-workers by Industry
(in %)

	Retailing	Other white collar	Manufac-turing	Other blue collar	Govern-ment
Addict co-workers	34	41	51	38	61
Pot smoking co-workers	44	56	66	49	68

Unlike several of the previous tables, the patterns in this one
are much the same for addict co-workers and pot smoking co-
workers. In each instance the government employees are in
front, closely followed by manufacturing employees, and retailing is at the bottom, closely followed by other blue-collar industries. Why government bureaucracies should be such a haven

for addicts and pot smokers is by no means clear. Perhaps
this reflects the difficulty of dismissing civil servants, or perhaps it reflects greater tolerance and permissiveness in the
public sector of employment. One other work characteristic
shows a slight relationship to drug use on the job, and that is
the measure of how strenuous the work is. Respondents whose
jobs were not at all strenuous were somewhat less likely to report addicts and pot smokers among their co-workers; but these
differences were only on the order of 6 percentage points.

Drug characteristics and drug users at work. In previous
chapters we have examined two measures of the addict's drug
world, the extent to which he was involved in drugs as measured
by the number of drugs he used, the amount he spent on drugs
and whether he used drugs at work, and the extent to which his
drug habit had an impact on his job. Both of these measures of
drug involvement are related to having colleagues who used
drugs. Table 6.6 shows the connection between drug involvement
and having co-workers who used drugs.

Table 6.6

Drug Users among Co-workers by Drug Involvement
of Addict Respondent (in %)

	Low	Medium	High
Addict co-workers	35	41	46
Pot smoking co-workers	33	53	62

As the addict's involvement with drugs increases, so does the
likelihood that some of his co-workers are addicts and smoke
pot. This clearly would suggest that the addict's own involvement with drugs is linked to the drug behavior of his co-workers.
Presumably the drug users among his work colleagues stimulate
the addict to become more deeply involved in drugs. This conclusion is born out by the data in Table 6.7, which links the index of the impact of drugs on the job to having colleagues who
use drugs.

Table 6.7

Having Drug Users among Co-workers by Impact of
Drugs on the Addict's Job
(in %)

	Low	Medium	High
Addict co-workers	35	45	45
Pot smoking co-workers	39	59	63

Both having fellow addicts as co-workers and having pot smoking co-workers are related to how much the addict's own habit affects his job. The more drug-using colleagues, the greater the impact of the addict's own habit on his job, again strong evidence of the social underpinnings of addiction and drug use. As in Table 6.6, the association is much stronger for pot smoking than for having addicts as colleagues. Pot smoking is no doubt a much more social activity than using heroin. Addicts are apt to go off by themselves to the restroom to use heroin, whereas pot smoking very much involves passing the joint from one smoker to another. The chances of getting high and having drugs affect work performance is probably greater for the on-the-job pot smoker than for the on- or off-the-job heroin user. In any event, the data of Table 6.7 support this conclusion.

The Visibility of the Addict's Habit

We have seen that at least 40% of the working addicts knew of at least one other addict at their place of work. This indicates that addicts in the same firm manage to communicate with each other about their habit. But how public this knowledge is at the work place is another matter. It might well be that addicts, because they belong to the same deviant culture of drugs, are able to communicate in subtle ways that nonaddicts do not understand. If so, then addicts might manage to keep their secret hidden from their nonaddict co-workers. The extent to which the addict's habit becomes public knowledge known to co-workers and bosses can be examined with the data on hand. The respondents were asked if their bosses knew they were using drugs and how many of their co-workers knew that they were on drugs.

The addict's habit is by no means a closely guarded secret unknown to straight people, for some 30% of the addicts reported that their bosses knew they were on drugs. The true percentage might well be higher in that some addicts probably were unaware that their bosses knew of their habit. As for co-workers, fully 62% of the respondents claimed that other people at their job, apart from bosses, knew of their drug habit. This is substantially more than the number reporting other addicts in their firm, and thus it is clear that many nonaddict co-workers knew of the addict's habit. Some 27% of the sample reported that one or two co-workers knew about their habit, 20% said that three to five co-workers knew, and 15% reported that six or more knew.

That almost a third of the addicts worked in settings where their bosses knew of their drug habit and almost two thirds in settings where co-workers knew forces an additional revision in the stereotype of working addicts. Not only are addicts able to hold jobs and perform them adequately in spite of their addiction, but many of them have come out of the closet in that their co-workers and bosses know of their habit. Apparently there is greater tolerance of the addict in the work place than the stereotype allows for. (We shall soon confront this matter of tolerance directly.)

Since the question about the boss knowing is strongly correlated with the question about co-workers knowing, we could have combined these items into an index of the visibility of the addict's habit; but these items did not always relate in the same way to other variables, and thus in the subsequent analysis we keep them separate. It is not surprising that knowledge of the addict's habit was much greater in work settings in which there were other people using drugs. The greater the drug problem at work as measured by the number of addicts and marijuana smokers, the more visible the addict to his fellow workers and employer. This can be seen from Table 6.8.

Table 6.8

Visibility of the Addict's Habit at Work by Having
Co-workers Who Are Addicts and Having
Co-workers Who Smoke Marijuana
(in %)

	Addict co-workers			Marijuana smoking co-workers		
	Low	Medium	High	Low	Medium	High
Boss knew	29	28	41	30	22	36
Co-workers knew	43	84	95	42	77	79
N =	(251)	(108)	(73)	(194)	(107)	(121)

The import of Table 6.8 is that addicts who are pretty much alone
as users are much more likely to keep their habit a secret than addicts who work with other addicts and drug users generally. Once
the addict finds some social support for his habit among co-workers
similarly addicted, his secret is likely to emerge and become public
knowledge. (The one deviant pattern is that the boss's knowledge
is unrelated to the frequency of marijuana use.)

Social characteristics and visibility at work. In the previous
section we saw that addicts with certain social characteristics
were more likely to work in establishments with other addicts.
This suggests that certain kinds of addicts migrate to work settings where they will find fellow deviants. If visibility of the
addict's habit is linked to his social characteristics, then we
might suppose that this is an artifact of the connection between
social characteristics and having co-workers as addicts, since,
as Table 6.8 shows, having addict co-workers contributes to
visibility. This chain of reasoning might well explain why the
men in our sample were more likely than the women to report
that their bosses and co-workers knew of their habit, since men
were much more likely to have co-workers who were also addicts. But having co-workers who are addicts does not explain
many of the associations between social characteristics and
visibility for the simple reason that the patterns differ for frequency of addicts and visibility of addiction. For example, on

the matter of religion, we saw that Protestants were more likely than either Jews or Catholics to have co-workers who were addicts, and Catholics more so than Jews. But when asked whether their boss knew they were addicted, the pattern is completely reversed. Now the Protestants are least likely to say yes (only 16%), and the Jews are most likely to say yes (47%), with the Catholics in between (35%). Similarly, ethnicity was not strongly related to working with other addicts and pot smokers, but ethnicity is related to visibility. Whites were more likely than blacks and Puerto Ricans to say that their bosses knew about their addiction, as can be seen from Table 6.9.

Table 6.9

Visibility of the Addict's Habit at Work by Ethnicity
(in %)

	White	Black	Puerto Rican
Boss knew	41	19	25
Co-workers knew	65	59	58

Although the whites lead the blacks and Puerto Ricans with regard to co-workers knowing as well, the difference is rather small. Much more pronounced is the pattern of the boss knowing. More than twice as many whites as blacks said their boss knew about their habit, and the gap is almost as great between the whites and Puerto Ricans. The reason for this finding is not at all obvious. Perhaps whites felt more secure in their jobs and were therefore not as discrete as nonwhites about their habit. Or perhaps the whites were more likely to seek help from their employers with regard to their habit. Although age was related to working with other addicts and pot smokers, it is not related to the visibility of the addict's habit, nor is education, another characteristic related to working with drug users. In short, we have found a rather different constellation of social characteristics to be related to visibility than to frequency of drug users.

   Work characteristics and visibility. Addicts who worked in
certain types of occupations were much more likely to have
their addiction known to their bosses and co-workers than addicts in other types of occupations. The addicts who were
craftsmen were particularly likely to have their addiction known
to others at work, whereas the lower white-collar workers were
least likely to have their habit known at work. For bosses the
craftsmen visibility rate was 42%, and for co-workers 74%. In
contrast, among the lower white-collar workers only 24% said
their bosses knew of their habit, and only 55% said that their
co-workers knew. The other occupational categories fell in between these extremes. One interpretation of this difference
rests upon the skill level of the occupation. Craftsmen are
highly skilled workers of great value to their employers. Their
skill level probably protects their job even when their employer
learns about their addiction. In contrast, lower white-collar
workers are relatively unskilled, with little job security; and
for this reason, addicts in such occupations probably go to great
lengths to hide their addiction.
   When industry is related to the visibility of the addict's habit
to his boss and colleagues, the results for government employees
differ from those of addicts employed in other industries. Government employees were least likely to say that their boss knew
of their habit: 24% compared with 34% of those employed in
other blue-collar industries, 30% of those employed in retailing,
and 26% of those employed in manufacturing and other white-
collar industries. But when it comes to co-workers knowing,
the government employees were much more likely to answer
affirmatively than those in other industries: 74% compared with
57% to 62% of those in other industries. Why should addicts
employed by government agencies share knowledge of their habit
with co-workers more than those in any other industry and at
the same time hide this knowledge from employers more successfully than those in other industries? Is this some kind of
statement about government employment fostering conspiracies
of co-workers against their bosses?
   One other characteristic of the addict's job turns out to be

related to visibility of his habit, and that is his income. The
more money the addict earned, the more likely were his boss
and his co-workers to know of his habit. This pattern is consistent for co-workers' knowledge and is evident for boss's
knowledge as well, as can be seen from Table 6.10.

Table 6.10

Visibility of the Addict's Habit by Weekly Income
(in %)

	Under $100	$100-149	$150-199	$200 and over
Boss knew	21	27	33	41
Co-workers knew	50	63	64	69

The meaning of the findings shown in Table 6.10 is by no
means clear. Craftsmen tend to earn more than those in other
occupations, and we have seen that their habit is most likely to
be known to others at work, a finding that we suggested might .
have something to do with their greater job security. Perhaps
job security is behind the income pattern as well. Those who
earn a great deal probably have more secure skilled jobs than
those who are poorly paid, and perhaps this explains why they
allow their co-workers to learn of their habit.

Drug involvement and visibility. We have seen that those who
were more involved in drugs and permitted their habit to affect
their work were more likely to work with other addicts. It turns
out that their addiction was also more visible to their co-
workers, as can be seen from the two parts of Table 6.11.

The strong associations between visibility and drug involvement and drug impact on work are not surprising. Those addicts who use drugs at work and have a heavy habit are not as
likely to be successful in hiding their habit as those with weaker
habits. Similarly, addicts whose work performances are affected by their taking drugs, for example, those who get high
during the workday or fall asleep on the job, are much more
likely to have their irregular behavior come to the attention of

Table 6.11

Visibility of the Addict's Habit by Drug Involvement
and Impact of Drugs on Work (in %)

| | Drug involvement | | |
	Low	Medium	High
Boss knew	17	25	36
Co-workers knew	44	56	74

| | Impact of drugs on work | | |
	Low	Medium	High
Boss knew	20	30	41
Co-workers knew	45	62	79

their colleagues and bosses than those whose habit has little
impact on their work performance. In sum, addicts who work
with other addicts, who are so dependent on drugs that they take
drugs during the working day and get high on the job, are the
very ones whose habit becomes visible to their co-workers and
superiors. But what are the costs of such visibility? How do
their bosses and co-workers who know of their habit feel about
it? It is to this question that we now turn.

The Attitudes of Work Associates
toward the Addict's Habit

We have seen that 30% of the addicts reported that their bosses
knew they were using drugs. What was the attitude of bosses
toward the addicts' habit? Did they disapprove? Did they tol-
erate the addiction? Or did they actually condone the habit and
even lend moral support to the addict? In fact, all three of
these reactions occurred with relatively similar frequencies.
Some 32% of those who said their boss knew reported that he
disapproved of their habit, and in the great majority of these
instances the disapproval took the form of being fired. Thus 35
of the 52 people who reported disapproval said they were fired.
In 5 cases the boss told the addict to stop working until he licked

his habit but that he could then have his job back, and in 11 cases
the boss did nothing but was very upset. These constitute the
subcategories of disapproval. In 33% of the cases where the
boss knew of the addict's habit, he did nothing and seemed to
ignore the situation. This tolerant reaction was reported by
54 addicts. Finally, some 56 addicts, 35% of the total who said
their boss knew, reported responses that we have classified as
sympathetic and supportive. In 33 cases the boss expressed
sympathy and did nothing, in 15 cases the boss helped the addict
enter a treatment program while he continued to work, and in
8 cases the boss actively participated in the addict's habit by
covering up for him, helping him to maintain his habit, and in
5 instances, joining the addict in the use of drugs.

The wide range of responses by bosses is repeated by the co-
workers. When asked what their co-workers thought of their
using drugs, the 62% who reported that their co-workers did
know were most likely to say that their co-workers did not seem
to care. Some 56% of this group gave the "did not care" response. Of the others, 24% reported that their co-workers disapproved of their drug habit, but incredibly enough, almost as
many, 20%, reported that their co-workers approved of their
drug behavior. Perhaps these were the cases where the co-
workers who knew were themselves addicts. The responses of
the bosses and co-workers have been combined into an index
that measures the climate of opinion at the work place about the
addict's habit. In constructing this index we have initially included those who reported that their co-workers or bosses did
not know about their habit. This index ranges from approval at
one end to disapproval at the other, with tolerance in the category immediately below approval and ignorance immediately before disapproval.*

The distribution of cases on this index of the attitudes of

---

*In constructing this index we had to make arbitrary decisions
about the cases in which the attitude of the boss was opposite to
the attitude of the co-workers. In these cases the boss's attitude
took precedence over the co-workers' attitude.

work associates toward the addict's habit is as follows:

	Total		Without "ignorance"
	N	%	%
Disapproval	88	16	25
Ignorance	171	32	—
Tolerance, do not care	168	31	45
Approval	111	21	30
	538	100	100

The surprising finding is that disapproval is the least likely response of work associates to the addict's habit. Somewhat more co-workers expressed approval than disapproval. The largest category consisted of co-workers who were ignorant of the addict's habit, 32% of the entire sample, closely followed by a tolerant attitude, that is, addicts reporting that their associates or bosses did not care one way or the other about their drug habit. The full distribution shown for everyone really contains two dimensions, knowledge of the addict's habit by either bosses or co-workers and the attitude of those who did know. The third column shows the distribution when the ignorance category is removed. When work associates did know of the addict's habit, their most typical response was tolerance or indifference, with almost half of the addicts whose associates knew giving this response. Strikingly, the approval response is somewhat more frequent than the disapproval response. This finding sheds considerable light on the situation of working addicts. One important reason why addicts were able to hold jobs for a relatively long period of time even though they were addicted is that they were not likely to meet with negative sanctions from their work associates, bosses, or co-workers. Most of the working addicts found considerable tolerance or active social support from their co-workers.

Whether work associates (boss and co-workers) approved, disapproved, or remained indifferent to the addict's habit (once they knew of it) turns out to be unrelated to the addict's social characteristics. Whether the addict is young or relatively old, white or black, male or female, well educated or poorly educated is not related to the response of work associates. The one exception to this rule seems to be religion, with Protestants reporting less disapproval from work associates than either Catholics or Jews (13% compared with 29% of the other two groups).

Neither occupation nor income is related to the attitude of work associates, but industry is associated with the kinds of colleague sanctions, as can be seen from Table 6.12.

Table 6.12

Attitude of Work Associates toward Addict's Habit
by Industry in Which Addict Worked
(in %)

Attitude	Retailing	Other white collar	Other blue collar	Manufacturing	Government
Disapproval	38	23	24	19	19
Not care	43	43	45	47	46
Approval	20	34	31	34	35
N =	(61)	(79)	(139)	(62)	(26)

Little difference among industries appears in the approval rates (last row), but there are some striking differences in disapproval rates. Addicts who worked in retailing were most likely to report disapproval from their colleagues, and those working in manufacturing and government were least likely to report disapproval, with those in other white-collar and other blue-collar industries falling in between. Why retailing should be so different from the other industries is not clear. Perhaps the need to interact with customers lowers the tolerance of co-workers for the deviance of the addict.

We have seen that many addicts reported that taking drugs at work had an impact on their job performance. They felt high at work, they sometimes fell asleep on the job, they sometimes missed work because of their drug habit, and they were prone

to accidents under the influence of drugs. When the drug habit
interferes with job performance, it is likely that supervisors
and co-workers would be less tolerant and more disapproving
of the addict's habit. The data on hand show this to be so
(Table 6.13).

Table 6.13

Attitude of Work Associates toward Addict's Habit
by Impact of Habit on the Job
(in %)

Attitude	Low	Medium	High
Disapproval	17	21	34
Not care	55	44	39
Approval	29	35	27
N =	(84)	(155)	(134)

The significant pattern emerges in the top row. The greater
the impact of the addict's habit on his job, the more likely he
is to meet with disapproval from his work associates. Tolerance of addiction declines markedly when the drug habit gets
in the way of the addict's work.

Not surprisingly, the attitude toward the addict's habit was
less disapproving in companies with a number of addicts among
the employees. As Table 6.14 shows, disapproval sharply declines as the number of addicts employed by the company
increases.

Table 6.14

Attitude of Work Associates toward Addict's Habit
by Frequency of Addicts in Company
(in %)

Attitude	Low	Medium	High
Disapproval	33	19	14
Not care	34	54	51
Approval	33	28	34
N =	(135)	(91)	(70)

The attitude of disapproval from work associates is more than twice as common in companies with hardly any addicts than in companies with a relatively large number of addicts. The prevalence of addicts in companies goes hand in hand with an attitude of tolerance toward addiction.

Dealing in Drugs at Work

One sign of the penetration of the drug culture in the work place is the extent to which drugs are bought and sold at work. The addicts in the sample were asked whether they themselves had bought drugs where they worked and whether they had sold drugs at work. These measures of drug dealing at work involve the addict himself. Had we asked whether drugs were bought and sold by anybody at work, undoubtedly many more would have responded affirmatively. In any case, 19% of the sample said they had bought drugs at work, and slightly more, 21%, said they had sold drugs at work. These questions are highly related to each other. Those who sold were much more likely to buy and vice a versa. When these questions are combined into an index of drug dealing at the work place, we find that two thirds of the sample were not involved in dealing at the work place, 22% either bought or sold, and 11% had done both.

Social characteristics and drug dealing. Dealing in drugs at work turns out to be related to a number of social characteristics. For example, men were much more likely to deal than women, 38% compared with 18%, and the better educated somewhat more than the poorly educated, as 30% of those with some college education dealt in drugs at work, 36% of those who were high school graduates, and only 29% of those who failed to graduate from high school. The two social characteristics most strongly related to dealing are age and ethnicity. Table 6.15 shows the relationship between age and dealing. Fully half of the youngest addicts bought or sold drugs at work compared with only a quarter of the oldest. Earlier we saw that older addicts held their jobs much longer than younger addicts, and perhaps abstaining from drug dealing is symptomatic of greater

job stability. But this finding could also mean that there is a
trend toward drug dealing at the work place, with the younger
addicts representing a more modern generation than the older
addicts.

Table 6.15

Those Dealing in Drugs (Buying or Selling)
at Work by Age (in %)

	17-21	22-24	25-29	30 plus
Dealing	51	38	29	25
N =	(71)	(141)	(203)	(140)

Whites were much more likely to deal in drugs at work than
Puerto Ricans, with blacks in between, as can be seen from
Table 6.16.

Table 6.16

Those Dealing in Drugs (Buying or Selling)
at Work by Ethnicity (in %)

	Whites	Blacks	Puerto Ricans
Dealing	39	30	21
N =	(228)	(220)	(98)

Almost two out of every five whites were involved in drug
deals at work, compared with less than a third of the blacks and
only a fifth of the Puerto Ricans.

Work characteristics and drug dealing. Occupation bears
some relationship to drug dealing. Those in the blue-collar
occupations were somewhat more likely to engage in buying or
selling drugs at work than those in white-collar occupations.
The craftsmen score highest in dealing with 39%, closely followed by the unskilled workers, 38%; at the other extreme are
the lower level white-collar workers, with only 28% involved in
dealing, and the higher white-collar workers are next lowest
with 31%.

We saw that addicts who were government employees were most likely to have their habit known to their co-workers, and they were least likely to meet with disapproval of their habit from their work associates. In keeping with those manifestations of a drug culture in government employment, we now learn that dealing in drugs was particularly prevalent among those who were government employees, as can be seen from Table 6.17.

Table 6.17

Those Dealing in Drugs (Buying or Selling) at Work
by Industry (in %)

	Government	Manufacturing	Other blue collar	Other white collar	Retailing
Dealing	53	35	33	30	28
N =	(34)	(85)	(204)	(133)	(90)

More than half of the government employees bought or sold drugs at work, a figure much larger than that of any other industry. In second place is manufacturing, with slightly more than a third of the addicts in that industry involved in dealing; and the industry with the lowest percentage of dealers is retailing, with only 28%. By all the indicators considered so far, government employment proves to be fertile territory for the drug culture. Is it possible that job security that stems from civil service encourages addicts who work for government to be less guarded about their habit in the work place? It must be remembered that our data deal only with the degree to which the addicts who worked in these different settings manifested their habit at work. We do not know from our data whether certain industries seem to generate more addicts than others. And as can be seen from the base figures, relatively few of the addicts we interviewed were employed in government, far fewer than any other category of industry. Thus government work may not be conducive to addicts, but the addicts who work there tend to manifest their habit in the work setting more than those in other industries.

Two other work characteristics bear some relationship to dealing. It turns out that the most poorly paid workers, those earning under $100 a week, were not nearly as likely to deal in drugs at the work place as those in higher paying jobs (only 19% compared with 34 to 41% in higher income categories). This suggests that there is little dealing in the poorest paid work settings because the workers do not have enough money to buy drugs from each other. The index of strenuousness of work bears a small relationship to drug dealing, with the percent of dealers climbing from 28 to 37 as the work becomes more strenuous. This might mean that workers with strenuous jobs feel they need drugs more at work. This would help explain the earlier finding that blue-collar work involves more dealing than white-collar work in that it tends to be more strenuous work.

Drug dealing at work is closely related to the number of drug users at work and the visibility of the addict's habit to his co-workers. That dealing is related to the frequency of users at work is hardly surprising: all this means is that where there is a market, transactions occur. This very strong relationship can be seen from Table 6.18, which relates dealing to the number of addicts in the company and the number of pot smokers in the company.

Table 6.18

Those Dealing by Number of Addicts in Company
and Number of Pot Smokers in Company

	Addicts in company			Pot smokers in company	
	%	N		%	N
Low	14	(253)	Low	12	(195)
Medium	50	(109)	Medium	46	(108)
High	64	(73)	High	55	(121)

In companies with a substantial number of drug users, dealing in drugs is the norm.

Dealing in drugs is related to whether the boss knew about the addict's habit (42% dealt where the boss knew and only 30% where the boss did not know) and is very strongly related to co-workers knowing. Among addicts whose co-workers knew of their habit, fully 48% bought or sold drugs, whereas only 8% bought or sold drugs where their co-workers did not know of their habit. This is hardly surprising, for the mere fact of dealing in drugs is a clue to co-workers that the dealer is himself a user, and probably an addict.

Drug dealing and the strength of the drug habit. Finally, dealing in drugs is strongly related to our measures of the degree of involvement in drugs. We have been dealing with two measures of involvement, one based on the number of drugs used and the amount of money spent on drugs, and the other with the extent to which the drug habit intrudes upon the addict's work performance, what we have called impact of drugs on work. As can be seen from Table 6.19, both of these measures are strongly related to dealing in drugs at work.

Table 6.19

Those Dealing in Drugs by Drug Involvement
and Impact of Drugs on Work

	Drug involvement		Impact of drugs on work	
	%	N	%	N
Low	9	(71)	19	(165)
Medium	28	(244)	32	(231)
High	44	(217)	50	(159)

The more involved the addict is in drugs, the greater his need to deal in drugs at the work place, that is, the less able he is to segregate his work life from his drug life.

Using Hard Drugs with Others at Work

Perhaps the ultimate symbol of a drug culture infiltrating the work place is for a group of co-workers to get together on the

job for the purpose of using drugs. When asked whether they
used drugs with co-workers on the job, 39% of the addicts responded affirmatively. It is hard to assess the significance of
this figure — is it high or low? The vast majority of working
addicts, as we have seen, used drugs while on the job. We now
know that a majority of them would shoot up by themselves.
This could mean that the majority did not have the opportunity
to use drugs with others because they did not know of other addicts at the place they worked. The 39% who did use drugs with
others is almost identical to the proportion who reported that
there were other addicts at the place they worked, 40% (see
Table 6.1).

Using drugs with others on the job is closely related to the
age of the addict. Younger addicts were much more likely to
use drugs with others at work than older addicts, the figure
being 52% in the youngest age group and steadily declining to
34% in the oldest age category. The only other social characteristic related to this attribute is sex. Men were much more
likely than women to participate in social sessions of drug taking
at work, 45% compared with 21%. Of the various work variables
we have considered, only industry is related to using drugs with
others at work. Just as the other information bearing on a drug
culture at work presented above suggested that government employment was fertile ground for a drug culture, so does this
item of using drugs with others. In the two white-collar categories (retailing and other white collar) approximately 35% reported using drugs with others at work. The two blue-collar
categories were much the same, with a rate of 40%. And again
government employment stands out with a rate of using drugs
with others of 47%.

The more deeply involved with drugs the addict was, as measured by the index of drug involvement and the index of the impact of drugs on his work, the more likely he was to use drugs
with others at the work place. These relationships can be seen
from Table 6.20. The relationships shown in Table 6.20 are
particularly strong. They call attention to the fact that the
working addicts are by no means of a piece. Some are much

more involved in the drug culture than others, and the more deeply involved they are, the more ready they are to create a drug culture at their place of work by making drug use at work a social event.

Table 6.20

Those Using Drugs with Others at Work by Drug
Involvement and Impact of Drugs on Job

	Drug involvement		Impact of drugs on job	
	%	N	%	N
Low	14	(71)	23	(164)
Medium	33	(242)	39	(230)
High	53	(217)	55	(159)

Not surprisingly, working addicts were much more likely to use drugs with others at work where the opportunity existed, that is, where there were other addicts at the work place. Table 6.21 shows how this variable is related to number of addicts and number of pot smokers at work.

Table 6.21

Those Using Drugs with Others at Work by Number of
Addicts at Work and Number of Pot Smokers at Work

	Addicts at work			Pot smokers at work	
	%	N		%	N
Low	18	(253)	Low	17	(195)
Medium	63	(108)	Medium	56	(108)
High	73	(73)	High	58	(120)

Drug socializing at work is more strongly related to the presence of other addicts at work than to the presence of pot smokers, as would be expected since the question refers to using hard drugs with others.

Finally, using drugs with others at work is very closely

related to dealing with others at work. Of those who neither
bought nor sold drugs at work, only 20% used drugs with others.
Of those who did either, drug socializing soars to 73%, and of
those who did both, the figure climbs still further to 86%. Dealing in drugs with others at work is virtually synonymous with
using drugs with others.

For a substantial minority of the addicts, their place of work
evolved into a setting as compatible with the drug culture as
the street corner. They were able to buy and sell drugs at work
and use drugs with others.

Learning about Drugs at Work

We close out this chapter on the intrusion of the drug culture
on the work place with data bearing a critical issue: the extent
to which the work place is a breeding ground for addicts. We
saw in an earlier chapter that most of the addicts in our sample
turned to drugs after they entered the job market and found a
full-time job. To what extent, then, did they learn about drugs
on the job? Did they pick up the habit in the neighborhoods in
which they lived, through their off-the-job peer groups, or did
they learn about drugs at the place where they worked? The
addicts were asked about this directly in the following question:
"Did you start using drugs for the first time on any job that you
had?" Some 16% of the addicts answered this question in the
affirmative. For them their jobs were the breeding grounds for
their habit, since they learned about drugs from their co-workers.

Two of the addict's social characteristics are moderately related to this variable, education and ethnicity. Those who went
to college were somewhat more likely to be introduced to drugs
at the work place than the less well educated, 24% compared
with 15 and 14%. This is not too surprising, for those who become addicts at an early age were not likely to go to college.
As for ethnicity, Puerto Ricans were more likely than whites
to learn about drugs through their jobs, 22% compared with 12%,
with blacks in between at 17%.

Being introduced to drugs through the work place is related

to both occupation and industry. The higher white-collar
workers, many of whom were paraprofessionals, were much
more likely than the others to learn about drugs through their
jobs; and in keeping with the previous findings, government employees were much more likely than those in other industries
to be introduced to drugs at the work place. These relationships
are shown in Table 6.22.

Table 6.22

Those Who Started Using Drugs on the Job by
Occupation and Industry

Occupation			Industry		
	%	N		%	N
Higher white collar	29	(45)	Retailing	11	(90)
Lower white collar	16	(174)	Other white collar	20	(133)
Craftsmen	20	(61)	Manufacturing	17	(85)
Semiskilled	16	(147)	Other blue collar	14	(204)
Unskilled	11	(125)	Government	29	(34)

Both the higher white-collar workers and those employed by
government show the same rate of 29%, a rate 9 percentage
points higher than the nearest competitor and 18 points higher
than the group at the opposite extreme.

One might suppose that working in a place that had addicts in
the work force would increase the risk of exposure to drugs at
work. But this variable is only weakly related to the number of
addicts in the firm, from 13% to 19% as we move from no addicts
to a fair number.

Some addicts thus learn about drugs through their jobs, and
this is more likely to happen to the higher white-collar workers
and those working in government.

Summary

   This chapter has examined the extent to which a drug culture has
intruded into the places where the addicts worked. We have seen
that many manifestations of a drug culture did indeed appear at

the work place. A substantial minority of addicts reported that at least some of their co-workers were addicts, and a majority reported marijuana use at the work place. The addict's condition was by no means kept secret from his co-workers. A substantial minority reported that their bosses knew of their addiction, and a majority reported that at least some co-workers knew. Most surprisingly, the work associates who knew of the addict's habit were rather tolerant. Not caring was the typical attitude, and there were as many who were supportive as were disapproving.

A minority of the addicts bought and sold drugs at the work place, and a substantial minority used drugs with co-workers on the job, sure signs of a drug culture infiltrating the work place. Unfortunately, we have no base line for assessing these figures. Had comparable research been done five or ten years ago, would the rates of such behavior at the work place have been significantly lower? And would a follow-up study five or ten years from now show much higher rates? Without such comparable data, we have no way of knowing whether there is a trend toward the drug culture moving in on the work place. But it must be remembered that our younger addicts were much more likely to be involved in these activities on the job than the older addicts, suggesting that there may indeed be such a trend. In any event, we have seen substantial evidence of the drug culture overlapping with the world of work.

7

Involvement in the Broader Drug Culture

In the last chapter we saw that for a substantial minority of
the working addicts, drug use at the work place was part of a
social experience. Thus about a third of the working addicts
bought or sold drugs at work, about 40% used drugs with their
co-workers at work, and a similar proportion knew of at least
one co-worker who was also an addict. In these respects ele-
ments of a drug culture had intruded in some work settings.
But a majority of the working addicts did not share drug experi-
ences at work. For this majority their drug habit was largely
hidden from their co-workers. Were those in this majority in-
clined to be "hidden addicts" at the time they were employed,
avoiding other addicts and shunning their style of life? Or did
these working addicts live pretty much a double life, participating in the straight world of work during working hours and in
the highly deviant world of other addicts and their drug culture
after working hours? The present chapter deals with this issue.

On the basis of the data on hand, most working addicts were
not "hidden addicts"; rather they led double lives in that they
were active participants in the broader drug culture. The idea
of a drug culture encompasses several things. Obviously, such
a culture presupposes social ties among addicts. Addicts must
hang out together and treat each other as friends if a drug culture is to emerge. Such a culture encompasses not only social
activities based on drugs but also the wide range of criminal
activities that addicts engage in to support their habit. To

111

engage in criminal behavior is to engage in behavior that, however deviant from the viewpoint of the dominant culture, is approved of by the drug culture. We have two sets of data bearing
on the addict's participation in the broader drug culture — his
reliance on crime to support his habit and his socializing with
other addicts. On the basis of these indicators, most of the
working addicts were active in the drug culture outside of work.
Thus 74% of the addicts told us that they resorted to crime to
help pay for their drug habit. Some stole from their employer
(either money or merchandise), 32%, and most stole outside of
work through various hustling activities (64%). Only 10% of the
working addicts claimed that they had no addict friends; 27% reported having some addict friends; and the majority, 64%, said
that most of their friends were addicts. When asked whether
they spent most of their nonworking hours with other addicts,
65% of the working addicts answered yes. A telling mark of
being a member of the broader drug culture is having a criminal
record. Most addicts must resort to crime, and most, sooner
or later, are arrested; this brush with the law becomes symbolic
of being part of a drug culture. In spite of the fact that they
worked and that many of them earned a fairly good living, a
majority of the working addicts had to resort to crime to support their habit, and a majority had a criminal record. Only
one fifth of the working addicts (19%) had avoided being arrested.
Some 81% had been arrested, and a majority, 59%, had been convicted of a crime. In the sections which follow we take a closer
look at these adpects of involvement in a drug culture.

Reliance on Crime to Support the Drug Habit

    Almost three out of every four working addicts told us that
they had to resort to crime to support their habit. This dependency on crime is virtually independent of the addict's social
characteristics. Whatever their age, education, religion, or
ethnicity, they resorted to crime in similar proportions. The
only exception is sex. Men were much more likely than women
to engage in criminal acts to support their habit (80% compared

with 58%). These negative findings hold not only for the question
of how the addict supported his habit, that is from earnings or
from crime, but also for the question of stealing from the employer and the question of hustling money outside of work. Engaging in criminal behavior is not related to most such work
characteristics as occupation, industry, job satisfaction, and
strenuousness of work. But there is one exception: income.
Those in the highest income group, because they earned so
much, were under less pressure to resort to crime. This can
be seen from Table 7.1, which presents the findings for the
three questions bearing on crime.

Table 7.1

Indicators of Criminal Behavior
(in %)

	Weekly income				
	Under $100	$100-149	$150-199	$200-249	$250 and over
Resort to crime	76	79	71	76	64
Steal from employer	37	40	36	42	39
Hustle outside work	62	66	65	70	56
N =	(105)	(220)	(122)	(50)	(56)

Engaging in crime in general and hustling outside of work fall
sharply among those earning over $250 a week, but, oddly
enough, stealing from the employer is as common among the
highest paid as those earning less (the middle row of Table 7.1).

Our earlier statement that criminal behavior is unrelated to
industry must be qualified in one important respect. Whether
the addict engages in crime at all is unrelated to industry, as
is stealing outside of the work place. But stealing from the employer is much more common in retail industry, where there is
an opportunity to take something of value, than in the other industries. Fully 61% of the addicts who worked in retailing stole
from their employer, compared with only 41 to 29% of those employed in other industries.

Although social characteristics and job characteristics are
generally not related to involvement in crime, the strength of
the addict's habit, as measured by the involvement in drugs index, and the degree of impact of drugs on the addict's job are
strongly related to dependence on crime. Those deeply involved
in drugs need so much money to support their habit, they cannot
get by on income legitimately earned. Table 7.2 shows the connection between drug involvement and these indicators of crime
involvement.

The great majority of those deeply involved with drugs engaged
in crime to support their habit (fully 86%), and as the data show,
the percent who stole from their employer and hustled outside
of work steadily increases with drug involvement.

Table 7.2

Indicators of Criminal Behavior by Involvement
with Drugs Index (in %)

	Low	Medium	High
Resort to crime	66	67	86
Steal from employer	27	34	49
Hustle outside work	52	60	73
N =	(71)	(242)	(215)

A similar pattern is shown by the other measure of drug involvement, the degree of impact of drug use on the addict's job
(Table 7.3).

Table 7.3

Indicators of Criminal Behavior by Impact of Drugs
on the Addict's Job (in %)

	Low	Medium	High
Resort to crime	68	72	85
Steal from employer	27	37	54
Hustle outside work	54	61	79
N =	(165)	(230)	(156)

Resorting to crime, whether stealing from the employer or stealing outside work, strongly increases as the impact of drugs on the addict's job increases. Those who get high at work, fall asleep at work, and miss work because of drugs are much more likely to be involved in crime.

The finding that involvement in crime is related to the impact of drugs on the addict's job suggests that there is an overlap between involvement in an on-the-job drug culture and the broader drug culture of the city. Further evidence of this overlap is provided by the strong association between buying or selling drugs at work and reliance on crime to support one's habit, as can be seen from Table 7.4.

Table 7.4

Indicators of Criminal Behavior by Dealing in
Drugs at the Place of Work (in %)

	Low	Medium	High
Resort to crime	71	78	89
Steal from employer	34	48	51
Hustle outside work	60	66	87
N =	(370)	(118)	(63)

The more likely the addict is to buy and sell drugs at work, the more likely he is to engage in criminal behavior both on and off the job to support his habit.

A similar picture of the overlap between a drug culture at work and the broader drug culture in the community is shown by the association between using drugs with others at work and involvement in criminal behavior (Table 7.5).

Table 7.5

Indicators of Criminal Behavior by Using Drugs
with Others at Work

	Use		Do not use	
	%	N	%	N
Resort to crime	80	(211)	71	(338)
Steal from employer	46	(214)	35	(339)
Hustle outside work	45	(210)	57	(334)

Socializing with Addicts

The second aspect of involvement in the broader drug culture
is socializing with other addicts. If working addicts were determined to be "hidden addicts," they would try to avoid other addicts and spend as little time with them as possible. But if their
mode of adjustment was to lead a double life, then they would
socialize with other addicts as part of their participation in the
broader drug culture. As we have seen, most working addicts
did socialize with other addicts. A majority told us that most
of their friends were addicts and that they spent most of their
nonworking time with other addicts.

In keeping with the notion that involvement in crime and socializing with other addicts are both aspects of the drug culture,
these two components are related to each other. Thus of those
who have no addict friends, 53% rely on crime to support their
habit, a figure that climbs to 69% of those who have some addict
friends and 80% of those with mostly addict friends.

Just as the addict's social characteristics had little bearing
on his criminal behavior, so they have no bearing on his socializing with other addicts. Whatever their age, education, religion,
ethnicity, or even sex, the addicts socialized with other addicts
to the same extent. The occupational variables are somewhat
more likely to be related to socializing with other addicts. Those
in higher white-collar occupations are least likely to say that
most of their friends are addicts (58%), the unskilled workers
are most likely to have mostly addict friends (71%), and government workers are least likely to spend most of their leisure
time with other addicts (50%), while those employed in manufacturing are most likely (69%). But again, the work variable that
has the most impact on participation in the broader drug culture
is income. Those in the highest income category are not only
least likely to be involved in crime, they are also least likely
to socialize with other addicts, as can be seen from Table 7.6.

The addicts in the highest income group were much less likely
to socialize with other addicts than those of lower income. It
would seem that the highest paid addicts, presumably because

Table 7.6

Socializing with Other Addicts by Weekly Income
(in %)

	Under $100	$100-149	$150-199	$200-249	$250 plus
Most friends are addicts	69	66	61	70	45
Spend most time with addicts	69	66	70	61	48
N =	(105)	(220)	(122)	(50)	(56)

of their adequate financial resources, were least dependent on
the drug culture and most successful at being "hidden addicts."
We saw that involvement in drugs was related to criminal behavior, and to some extent drug involvement is also related to
socializing with other addicts. Table 7.7 shows that drug involvement is strongly related to spending most free time with
other addicts but only slightly related to having mostly addict
friends.

Table 7.7

Socializing with Other Addicts by Drug Involvement
(in %)

	Low	Medium	High
Most friends are addicts	62	61	67
Spend most time with addicts	45	66	71
N =	(71)	(244)	(217)

The other measure of involvement with drugs, the extent to
which the addict's habit had an impact on his job, is more
strongly related to socializing with other addicts, as can be
seen in Table 7.8. The import of Tables 7.7 and 7.8 would seem
to be that those most strongly hooked on drugs are also the ones
most deeply enmeshed in the addict culture.

Table 7.8

Socializing with Other Addicts by Impact of Drugs on Job
(in %)

	Low	Medium	High
Most friends are addicts	61	59	72
Spend most time with addicts	52	66	79

We have seen that dealing in drugs at work was related to involvement in crime suggesting an overlap between participating in a drug culture at work and in the broader drug culture. Oddly enough, however, dealing in drugs at work is not related to socializing with other addicts. Having most friends who are addicts and spending most free time with addicts do not increase the likelihood of buying or selling drugs at work. But there is one respect in which socializing with other addicts does contribute to the drug culture at work. Working addicts who socialize primarily with other addicts are more likely to be visible to their co-workers. The questions about whether the employer knew of the addict's addiction and whether his co-workers knew have been combined into a knowledge index. As Table 7.9 shows, this index is related to socializing with other addicts.

Table 7.9

Socializing with Other Addicts by Co-Workers'
Knowledge of Addict's Habit (in %)

Knowledge index	Addict friends		
	None	Some	Most
Low	43	37	27
Medium	34	41	40
High	23	23	33
N =	(53)	(150)	(352)

Although the relationship is not particularly strong, it would seem that having addict friends contributes to the addict's habit becoming public knowledge. In other words, addicts who are deeply involved in the broader drug culture are not as likely to remain "hidden addicts" as those who eschew the community's drug culture.

Having a Criminal Record

We have seen that in spite of their being gainfully employed, most of the working addicts had to resort to crime to support their habit. It comes as no surprise that the great majority have an arrest record and that a majority were convicted of crimes. Thus 80% had been arrested, and 59% convicted. Only 20% of the working addicts were able to avoid being arrested.

Although resorting to crime was not related to most of the social characteristics we have been considering, having a criminal record is related to a number of these characteristics. For example, age is very much related to having been convicted of a crime, as can be seen from Table 7.10.

Table 7.10

Having a Criminal Record by Age
(in %)

Criminal record	17-21	22-24	25-29	30 plus
Never arrested	14	28	21	10
Arrested only	38	25	23	9
Convicted	48	47	56	81
N =	(71)	(141)	(203)	(140)

The conviction rate steadily increases with age, almost doubling among the 30 and over group when compared with the 17 to 21 year olds. To get arrested and convicted is clearly a hazard of the addict world, and the longer one is an addict, the more likely one is to get caught at crime. The telling point about Table 7.10 is that this holds true even for addicts who were able to hold a job for a number of years, as many in the oldest age group were able to do.

We saw that committing crimes is unrelated to the amount of education the addicts had. Those who attended college were as likely to resort to crime as those who failed to graduate from high school. But having an education is clearly an aid in avoiding the criminal justice system. As Table 7.11 shows, the better educated were less likely to get arrested, and especially less likely to get convicted than the poorly educated.

Table 7.11

Having a Criminal Record by Education
(in %)

Criminal record	Some high school	High school graduate	Some college
Never arrested	14	23	28
Arrested only	22	24	20
Convicted	64	53	52
N =	(292)	(154)	(109)

Just as education relates to unequal treatment at the hands of the criminal justice system, so does religion. We saw that there was little difference between the three major religious groups with regard to participation in crime. But the relatively few Jewish addicts were much less likely to come in contact with the law than the Protestant and Catholic addicts. Thus 35% of the Jewish addicts were never arrested, compared with 24% of the Protestants and only 16% of the Catholics. Only 38% of the Jews were ever convicted of a crime, in contrast with 57% of the Protestants and 61% of the Catholics. Sex is strongly related to having a criminal record. Men were much more likely than the women to have been arrested and convicted of crimes. Thus only 12% of the men managed to avoid an arrest, compared with 39% of the women; and 68% of the men were convicted of crimes, compared with 32% of the women. Ethnicity is about the only social characteristic not related to a criminal record. White addicts are as likely as blacks and Puerto Ricans to have been arrested and convicted.

We saw that industry was unrelated to criminal acts, but striking differences arise among industries with respect to having a criminal record. The addicts who worked in blue-collar industries were much more likely to have been arrested and convicted than those who worked in white-collar industries, and government employees were especially successful in avoiding convictions (Table 7.12).

Table 7.12

Having a Criminal Record by Industry of Employment
(in %)

Criminal record	Govern-ment	Retail-ing	Other white collar	Manufac-turing	Other blue collar
Never arrested	27	21	26	18	13
Arrested only	35	26	25	15	19
Convicted	38	53	50	67	69
N =	(34)	(90)	(133)	(85)	(204)

Government employees are only slightly more likely than those employed in white-collar industries to avoid arrest, but they are much more successful in avoiding conviction. Blue-collar workers, by contrast, were especially likely to be arrested and convicted. Their conviction rate is more than twice that of the government employees. Inasmuch as industry was not related to participating in crime, it would seem that Table 7.12 calls attention to another inequity in the criminal justice system.

Occupation shows a pattern similar to industry. Although occupation was not strongly related to participation in crime, those in white-collar occupations were more likely to avoid arrest and conviction than those in blue-collar occupations. Thus about a quarter of the higher and lower white-collar workers were never arrested, compared with 13% of the craftsmen, 18% of the semiskilled, and 7% of the unskilled. Only about half of the white-collar workers were convicted, compared with 59% of the craftsmen, 64% of the semiskilled, and fully 79% of

the unskilled. Arrest and conviction rates thus vary inversely
with occupational prestige, a further sign of inequality in the
criminal justice system.

We saw that the working addicts who earned the most money,
those who made over $250 a week, did not resort to crime as
often as those who earned less. Surprisingly, income is in no
way an antidote to brushes with the law for these working addicts. If anything, the relationship is curvilinear, with the
lowest paid and the highest paid having somewhat lower arrest
records, as can be seen from Table 7.13.

The pattern is extremely irregular. Thus those in the second-
lowest and second-highest income categories have the highest
arrest and conviction records, and those who earned the most
do not do as well as those who earned the least. What is particularly strange about these results is that the highest income
group is the only one which is more likely to have an arrest
record than to have resorted to crime to support their habit.
Thus 64% of those who earned over $250 a week engaged in
crime to support their habit, but 73% of this group had an arrest record. This would suggest that this highest income group
contains people who were arrested for reasons unrelated to
their drug habit.

Table 7.13

Criminal Record by Weekly Income

Criminal record	Under $100	$100-149	$150-199	$200-249	$250 plus
Never arrested	26	16	19	12	27
Arrested only	25	20	25	24	18
Convicted	50	65	57	64	55

One job characteristic that failed to relate to most of the attributes we have considered in this report turns out to be
strongly related to having a criminal record, and that is how
strenuous the addict's job was. Of those whose job was not at
all strenuous, 24% managed to avoid being arrested; of those

whose job was very strenuous, only 12% avoided arrest. Conversely, 48% of those in nonstrenuous jobs were convicted, compared with fully 72% of those in very strenuous jobs. This pattern holds even though there was very little difference between these groups with regard to engaging in crime. (Those whose jobs were very strenuous were 6 percentage points more likely to engage in crime, 77% compared with 71%.) We have seen that blue-collar workers were more likely than white-collar workers to have a criminal record, and since blue-collar work is more strenuous, part of this pattern may be due to the inequalities in the criminal justice system. But it is also likely that this finding reflects the differential impact of a criminal record on finding employment. People with criminal records are apt to be barred from certain occupations and industries. To the extent that strenuous work is held in disfavor, barriers to such jobs are no doubt lowered to the point where those with criminal records are eligible.

We have seen that drug involvement and having drugs affect one's job were related to participation in the broader drug culture, including participation in crime. Not surprisingly, those more deeply involved in drugs were more likely to have a criminal record. Table 7.14 shows how these measures are related to the likelihood of being convicted of a crime.

Table 7.14

Those Convicted of a Crime by Drug Involvement
and Impact of Drugs on Job

Index score	Drug involvement		Impact of drugs on job	
	%	N	%	N
Low	49	(71)	52	(165)
Medium	59	(244)	61	(231)
High	62	(217)	62	(159)

As involvement with drugs increases, so does the probability of conviction.

Those who were part of a drug culture at their place of work were also more likely to have a criminal record. Table 7.15 shows the connection between dealing in drugs at work and having a record.

Table 7.15

Criminal Record by Dealing in Drugs at Work
(in %)

Criminal record	No dealing	Buy or sell	Buy and sell
Never arrested	23	14	8
Arrested only	22	23	21
Convicted	55	63	71
N =	(372)	(120)	(63)

Two other measures of a drug culture at the work place are also related to having a criminal record. Working addicts who knew of addicts among their co-workers were more likely to have a criminal record than those who did not know of any other addicts at their place of work (the conviction rate rises from 54% to 60-66% as the number of addict co-workers increases). And addicts who used drugs with others at the work place were more likely to have been convicted of crimes than those who did not (65% compared with 55%).

Needless to say, the more deeply enmeshed the working addict was in the broader drug culture, the more likely he was to have a criminal record. This is evident from the data on socializing with other addicts. Of those who claimed that they had no addict friends, 34% were never arrested; of those who said they had some addict friends, 21% were never arrested; and this rate drops to 16% of those who said that most of their friends were addicts. Conversely, the conviction rate increases from 47% to 58-61% as the number of addict friends increases. A similar pattern appears when spending most free time with addicts is related to having a criminal record. Of those who did not spend most of their time with addicts, 25% avoided an arrest, but only 16% of those who did spend most of their time with other addicts escaped arrest. Similarly, the likelihood of conviction increases (53% compared with 62%).

Not surprisingly, having a criminal record is strongly related to reliance on crime to support one's drug habit. Those who resorted to criminal acts, who stole from their employer, and who hustled outside work were much more likely to have been arrested and convicted of crimes. But what is surprising, astonishingly so, is that a substantial majority of those who did not resort to crime to support their habit also had an arrest record. These findings appear in Table 7.16.

Table 7.16

Arrest Record by Resorting to Crime
to Support Habit, Stealing from Employer,
and Hustling outside Work

Response	Resorted to crime to support habit		Stole from employer		Hustled outside work	
	%	N	%	N	%	N
Yes	86	(410)	85	(216)	89	(350)
No	66	(141)	78	(339)	66	(196)

Reading down each column we see the obvious fact that engaging in crime is related to having a criminal record. But the surprising finding is shown by the figures in the second row. In every instance a majority of those who did not resort to crime to buy their drugs nevertheless had an arrest record. This does not mean that police are more ready to arrest addicts even when they are not guilty of any offense, for substantial numbers of those who claimed that they did not engage in crime to support their habit were convicted of crimes. Thus 43% of those who did not resort to crime to support their habit, 54% of those who did not steal from their employer, and 44% of those who did not hustle were still convicted of crimes. This strongly suggests that addicts, whether they work or not, are part of the criminal culture of the community and may well commit crimes independent of their drug habit.

To summarize the findings presented so far, we have seen
that most working addicts participate in the broader drug culture in that they socialize with other addicts and engage in crime
to support their habit. This need to turn to crime to pay the in-
flated prices of illegal drugs partly explains why the marriage
these addicts attempted between their drug habit and the world
of work eventually broke down. Most of the working addicts had
criminal records, and this fact, as much as anything else, drove
them out of the labor force. When asked their reasons for leaving their job, the great majority who had left their job by the
time we interviewed them gave a variety of reasons. Some 17%
said they were fired and did not explain why. Conceivably, some
of them were fired because of their brushes with the law. An
additional 6% said they were laid off and 4% said their firm went
out of business. The percent who left work unvoluntarily because
of actions by their employer thus comes to 28. Interference
from the drug habit was given as the main reason for quitting
by 14% of the addicts. This is the commonly held view of the
incompatability of drugs and work, but it applies to only one out
of every seven of the working addicts. An additional 7% said
that they quit their job in order to enter a drug treatment program, and this answer too points to the drug habit as a reason
for quitting. In all then, 21%, or one in every five, mentioned
their drug habit as the reason for their leaving their job. But
almost as many, some 17%, referred to their criminal activities
as the reason for their leaving their job. Thus 12% said they
lost their job because they were arrested, 3% said they lost
their job because they were caught stealing, and 2% said they
quit their job so that they could devote more time to their criminal activities. Other reasons for quitting included personal
problems, illness, and pregnancy. But the critical point is that
a substantial number lost their job because of their involvement
in the broader drug culture of crime.

8

Summary and Conclusions

This report has dealt with a deviant group within a deviant population: addicts who managed to hold full-time jobs in spite of their addiction. Its concern has been with how these addicts were able to integrate their drug habit with the world of work and the various ways in which their drug habit intruded upon their jobs.

We began by examining the social characteristics of these working addicts in comparison with those of addicts in treatment programs and the general population of nonaddicts. Although our sample of working addicts was selected from drug treatment programs, we found that these working addicts differed in significant respects from all addicts in treatment programs and were more like the general nonaddict population than most addicts were. For example, they tended to be older, better educated, and more often married than the general addict population, and most significantly, they were much more likely to be white than the addict population in treatment, which is composed primarily of members of minority groups. On the basis of these comparisons, we were able to conclude that the missing group, working addicts not in treatment programs, the so-called "hidden addicts," were probably even more like the general population than our sample of working addicts in treatment programs. These findings are a sharp reminder of the dangers of generalizing from addicts in treatment programs. Addicts in treatment are addicts who have failed in adjusting to their habit. For a

number of years the addicts we sampled were able to hold jobs
while they were addicted, and during this time they were successful in blending their habit with a more normal life. Eventually they failed, and most left their jobs and all entered treatment programs. Addicts who never worked might be thought of
as double failures; and since they make up the bulk of the addicts
in treatment programs, their social characteristics provide a
picture of failed addicts rather than the entire addict population.
Unfortunately, there are no data on the number of addicts not in
treatment programs. Whether this number is small or large
relative to the number in treatment is a critically important
issue for the question of what kinds of people become addicts.
If the number of hidden addicts is small, then addicts in general
may well come disproportionately from the underclasses of the
poorly educated minority groups. But if the number of "hidden
addicts" is large, then the addict population may not be too different from the general population. At any rate, we have seen
that those addicts who were able to integrate their drug habit
with the world of work were more likely to have the attributes
of the dominant majority of nonaddicts than were most addicts
in treatment.

In Chapter 2 we considered the nature of the addicts' drug
habit. Conceivably, these addicts were able to hold jobs because
they were only marginally involved in drugs; and if they had a
strong dependency on drugs, they would have been unable to
work. The data on hand, however, indicated that most working
addicts had a fairly heavy habit. Almost all of them were addicted to the drug that is considered most damaging, heroin,
and most of them were using more than one drug. Thus fully
61% were polydrug users, and more than one in every five used
at least three illegal drugs besides marijuana. Most of them
(82%) were so dependent on drugs that they had to use drugs
during the working day, and a substantial number had an expen-
sive habit. Thus more than one in every five spent more than
$50 a day on their habit, and more than half (55%) spent more
than $25 daily on illegal drugs. When these indicators of drug
dependency were combined in an index, we found that only 16%

scored low on drug involvement, 63% were in the middle group, and 21% scored high. In short, most working addicts managed to hold full-time jobs in spite of having fairly strong drug habits.

Chapter 3 examined in some detail the labor force participation of the working addicts. We saw that their occupations were fairly similar to those of the general population with one exception. Substantially fewer were located in the higher white-collar occupations of professionals, managers, and administrators. One reason for this is that the working addicts were not as well educated as the general population, and higher education is a requirement for entry into the professions and most managerial positions. But another reason for the underrepresentation of the professions in the sample is that we have dealt with working addicts in treatment programs, that is, working addicts who eventually failed and had to come out of the closet. Had we been able to sample "hidden addicts," that is, currently successful addicts, the professions would no doubt be well represented. The working addicts had been employed in a variety of industries, including government, but they were most heavily concentrated in retailing and manufacturing. In terms of income, the working addicts compared quite favorably with the general population. Information on the income of the general population came from the 1970 census, and because of inflation, the working addicts in 1974 and 1975 earned substantially more than the general population had in 1970. When inflation is discounted, it would seem that the addicts earned at least as much as the general population. Some of the working addicts were extremely well off financially, having been owners of their own business, entertainers, or employees in the lucrative construction trades. In terms of their occupations and income, a number of working addicts occupied middle-class positions in the social hierarchy. In short, they were by no means confined to the lower reaches of the class structure. In spite of their drug habit, many of these addicts held their job for some time. Some 68% of the addicts held their job for a year or more, 43% for two or more years, 28% for three or more years, and 15% for four or more years. Clearly, addiction did not prevent many of these addicts

from enjoying job stability. From a variety of questions, it
was determined that most addicts were well satisfied with their
jobs, a further indication of their successful integration into the
world of work.

Considerable variation was found within the sample of working
addicts. For example, the white addicts had better occupations
and substantially more income than the black and Puerto Rican
addicts. Whites and the young were much more heavily involved
in drugs than members of minority groups and the older addicts.
And job satisfaction was greater among the higher white-collar
workers and craftsmen than among the other occupation groups,
and job satisfaction was strongly correlated with income.

Chapter 4 considered the connections between job characteristics and drug involvement. The most significant finding to
emerge from this analysis was that drug involvement increased
sharply with income. The more money the working addict
earned, the more money he spent on drugs, the more drugs he
used, and the more dependent he was on drugs during the working day. This finding strongly suggests that the degree of involvement with drugs is determined largely by opportunity. If
an addict can afford it, he will use a lot of drugs. And conversely, using a lot of drugs is apparently no deterrent to high
earnings. Since income is related to better-quality jobs and
length of employment, it can be taken as a measure of success
in the occupational world. That income is related to drug involvement thus suggests that the more successful the addict
was in the world of work, the more dependent he became on
drugs. This finding strongly suggests that there is no basic incompatability between having a job and having a drug habit.

Chapter 5 examined the impact of the addict's habit on his
job. We saw that most addicts used drugs at work, and a majority (54%) got high from drugs at work. But getting high was
not the primary reason for taking drugs. Most working addicts
took drugs at work to avoid sickness, although many admitted
that taking drugs at work made them feel good too. About a
quarter of the working addicts admitted that taking drugs at
work sometimes caused them to fall asleep on the job, and more

than half (53%) said that their drug habit caused them to lose days of work. These items were combined into an index of the impact of drugs on the job, and it was found, not surprisingly, that those more deeply involved in drugs were also more likely to have drugs affect their job. In spite of the fact that most of the working addicts did take drugs at work and did experience some effect of the drugs while on the job, their job performance apparently did not suffer. Most addicts (64%) claimed that their supervisors thought they were doing very well on their job, and almost as many (62%) gave themselves this high rating. But drugs did have a deleterious effect on the job performances of some of the addicts. About 5% of the working addicts said that they had injured themselves, 4% had injured someone else because of their being on drugs, and 7% said they had damaged equipment because they had been high on drugs.

Chapter 6 examined the social context of drug use on the job. To what extent had a drug culture intruded upon the work place? We saw that 40% of the working addicts claimed that one or more of their co-workers were also addicts. More than 60% of the addicts said that at least some of their co-workers knew of their habit, and more than a third said that their boss knew of their habit. For a substantial majority then, their habit was known at their work place. What was a particularly surprising finding was the attitude of co-workers and supervisors to the addict's habit. Of those who reported that their habit was known to co-workers or their boss, only 25% reported that these work associates disapproved of their habit, almost half (45%) claimed that their work associates did not care one way or the other, and 30% reported that their co-workers were sympathetic and even approving of their drug habit.

Not only did a substantial minority of addicts have a work associate who shared their habit and not only was the addict's habit fairly visible to co-workers, but signs of a drug culture in the work place were even more evident for a number of the working addicts. Thus about a third of the working addicts said they bought or sold drugs at their place of work, and even more, almost 40%, said they used drugs with co-workers during the

working day. Thus a number of work settings in New York City,
and most likely other cities as well, have come to harbor drug
cultures created by their employees.

Chapter 7 dealt with the issue of the involvement of working
addicts in the broader drug culture of the community, a community characterized by criminal activities and close social ties
among fellow addicts. Were the working addicts "hidden addicts"
during their time in the labor force, we might suppose that they
would avoid other addicts and that they would be able to support
their habit from their earnings. But the data of Chapter 7
showed that these working addicts were very much involved in
the broader drug culture and that they had led double lives, participating in the straight world during the working day and the
addict world after hours. Thus the great majority told us that
even though they earned money, they still had to resort to crime
to support their habit. Most of the working addicts had mostly
fellow addicts as friends, and most of them spent most of their
nonworking time in the company of other addicts. The great majority of these working addicts had criminal records. Fully 81%
had been arrested, and 59% had been convicted of crimes. To a
large extent the criminal records of these addicts stemmed from
their need to resort to crime to support their habit. But perhaps
the most telling finding of Chapter 7 was that even those addicts
who did not have to resort to crime to support their habit were
likely to have criminal records. Thus while they were not as
likely to have been arrested and convicted as those who did
have to steal to support their habit, a majority of them had been
arrested, and a substantial minority had been convicted of
crimes. This finding points to an affinity between crime and
drugs that transcends the need to steal to support the drug habit.
Those who, for whatever reason, turn to crime are perhaps more
susceptible to drug abuse than those who stay clear of criminal
activity. But by the same token, those who turn to drugs and become addicted find that sooner or later they must turn to crime
to support their habit. The connection between crime and drugs
is thus a two-way street.

Their involvement with the criminal justice system turns out

to be an important factor in the ultimate failure of these working addicts in the world of work. Many addicts had to leave
their jobs because they were involved in crime.

The findings presented in this report have a number of implications. First, the stereotype of the addict as a person who
is highly unstable and even sick, too unstable and sick to hold
a job, must be revised. Many addicts were successful in holding jobs for a substantial period of time, a year or more while
addicted. Their work apparently did not suffer because of their
habit, as most felt their bosses would rate their job performance
highly, and most reported that their co-workers, including their
bosses, were tolerant and even sympathetic toward their drug
habit, an attitude not likely to exist if the working addict was
failing at his job. If addiction is not as incompatible with work
as first supposed, then why did these working addicts eventually
leave their jobs and enter treatment programs? It is our considered judgment, on the basis of the findings, that one major
reason for the eventual failure of these working addicts is that
their habit is illegal. In order to obtain the drugs they need,
these addicts have to enter the drug culture and become crimi-
nals. Were the United States to have a system like that in
England, where the addict is treated as a medical case and
given the drugs needed to sustain him, it is quite likely that
most addicts would be able to find jobs, and most addicts would
be able to keep their jobs in spite of their habit.

The findings of this study suggest that much can be learned
by carrying out experiments whereby some addicts would be
provided with free drugs in the quantity to which they have become accustomed, to see whether they can lead successful lives
in the world of work. Such an experiment might go far beyond
the current methadone maintenance programs with regard to
type of drug and dosage. If the findings of the current study are
valid, then it would seem that such experiments would show that
addicts can survive and prevail in the world of work. Given the
tremendous cost of the current patterns of drug abuse in our
society based on the illegality of drugs, such experiments have
much to recommend them.

Finally, the findings of this study call attention to the need
for further research. One major gap in our knowledge concerns
the "hidden addicts," those who lead relatively normal lives
even though they are addicted to drugs. Would research show
that these hidden addicts perform well in the job world, or does
their habit manage to undermine their role performances? Research also is needed on the relative harm of drug addiction
and alcoholism for the world of work. Our data suggested that
working addicts managed rather well in their jobs. Is the same
true of alcoholics, or does their job performance suffer more
drastically because of their addiction? Currently, society treats
drug addiction as a much more serious social problem than alcoholism. But until the comparative studies are made and the
costs of alcoholism compared with the costs of drug addiction,
effective policies cannot be formulated.

APPENDIX 1

Treatment Programs

Methadone Maintenance Treatment Programs

	Number of interviews
Albert Einstein College of Medicine	49
Greenwich House	39
Kings County Addictive Disease Hospital	132
Mora Narcotic Rehabilitation Foundation	125
Mt. Sinai Hospital	50
Total	395

Residential Therapeutic Communities

	Number of interviews
Daytop Village, Inc.	75
Integrity House	21
Project Return	23
Salvation Army	20
Samaritan House	21
Total	160
Total number of interviews	555

APPENDIX 2

Questionnaire

1. During the time you were addicted to drugs, did you ever
   have a full-time job for at
   least three months?

                                    Yes____
                                    No____

   IF NO: TERMINATE INTERVIEW

2. How old were you when you
   had your first full-time job?

                              Exact age____

3. How old were you when you
   knew that you were addicted
   to drugs?

                              Exact age____

4. Where were you when you
   found out that you were addicted to drugs, in New York,
   Puerto Rico, the military, or
   where?

                           New York____
                        Puerto Rico____
                           Military____
                    Other (Where?)____
                        _____

141

IF MILITARY:
A) Where were you stationed?

Vietnam_____
Other overseas_____
Stateside_____

5. How many different full-
time jobs have you had?

#_____

6. What was the first full-time
job you had?

_____

(IF APPROPRIATE, ASK Q. 7 AND 8)

7. What was your next full-time job?

_____

8. What was your last full-time job
before you came into this program?

_____

(ASK OF EVERYBODY)

9. What was the longest full-time job you
had while you were addicted? (Prior to
Program Methadone)

_____
(WHAT WAS THE SPECIFIC OCCUPATION)

10. Of all the jobs you had, which one
did you like the best?

_____

Now I want to ask you some questions about
the job you had the longest (JOB LISTED IN Q. 9)

11. What was the name of the company
for which you worked?

_____
(NAME OF COMPANY)

12. What kind of company was that?

_____
(NAME OF INDUSTRY)

13. Where in the company did you work?
(e.g., mail room, stock room, computer, sales, etc.)

_____

14. When did you first go to work   _____/_____
for that company?   Month   Year

15. Are you still working for that company?

Yes_____
No_____

IF NO:
A) How long did you have that job?

___yrs. ___mos.

16. Did you find the work that you
did interesting; was it dull or
was it in between?

Interesting_____
Dull_____
In between_____

17. Did that job involve hard
physical work?

Yes_____
No_____

18. Did the work require you to get
    dirty, or did you stay clean
    during the working day?

                                     Get dirty_____
                                     Stay clean_____

19. Was the work you did in any
    way dangerous?

                                           Yes_____
                                            No_____

20. Did you pretty much decide how to
    do your work, or did you have to
    follow closely the orders of
    other people?

                               Decided for self_____
                               Followed orders_____

21. Apart from lunch, how much time
    did you have for yourself each
    working day, including coffee breaks?

                                        None _____
                             Up to half-hour _____
                           Half-hour to 1 hour _____
                           More than one hour _____

22. How good were your chances to get
    ahead on that job? Very good, fairly
    good, or not too good?

                                    Very good_____
                                   Fairly good_____
                                   Not too good_____

23. How much did you like that job —
    a lot, a little, or did you hate it?

                                   Liked a lot_____
                                 Liked a little_____
                                      Hated it_____

24. What was your highest salary
    on that job?

$_____per hour
$_____per week
$_____per month
$_____per year

25. Since you were addicted to drugs
    while you were working on that
    job, why didn't you quit the job?

26. During the time you had that job, were you using
    (READ OFF EACH DRUG FROM LIST)?

    (FOR EACH DRUG USED, ASK Q. 27)

27. Were you using_____while at work?

DRUG	USING			WORKING DAY	
	Yes	No		Yes	No
Heroin	1	2	(56)	1	2
Street Methadone	1	2	(58)	1	2
Program Methadone	1	2	(60)	1	2
Barbiturates	1	2	(62)	1	2
Amphetamines	1	2	(64)	1	2
Cocaine	1	2	(66)	1	2
Alcohol	1	2	(68)	1	2
Other (What?)	1	2	(70)	1	2

IF NONE OF THESE DRUGS WERE TAKEN DURING
WORKING DAY, ASK Q. 28 AND 29.

28. Did you take any other drug during the
    working day to help you get through the day?

Yes_____
No_____

IF YES:
A) What drugs did you take?

_____

29. Did you take any drugs just before
    going to work?

                                          Yes_____
                                           No_____

    IF YES:
    A) Which drugs did you take?

    _____

IF ONE OR MORE DRUGS TAKEN DURING WORKING
DAY, ASK Q. 30-35, IF NONE, SKIP TO Q. 36.

30. Did you take these drugs on the
    job to avoid being sick, to feel
    good, to get high, or what?

                            Avoid sickness_____
                                Feel good_____
                                Get high_____
                            Other (What?)_____

                            _____

                                          DECK II

    (IF NOT ALREADY LEARNED IN Q. 30, ASK Q. 31)

31. Did taking these drugs on the job
    make you high in any way?

                                          Yes_____
                                           No_____

IF YES:
A) Did you do anything to keep other
   people from noticing the effect of
   the drug on you?

                                          Yes_____
                                          No_____

IF YES:
1. What did you do?

_____

32. How many times a day would you
    take these drugs on the job?   #_____

33. Where would you go to take this
    drug on the job?

_____

34. Did taking drugs on the job make it
    harder for you to do your job, did it
    make the job easier, or did it have
    no effect?

                                       Harder_____
                                       Easier_____
                                    No effect_____

35. Did taking drugs on the job ever
    cause you to fall asleep in the
    rest room or something like that?

                                          Yes_____
                                          No_____

ASK Q. 36 ON OF ALL RESPONDENTS

36. How good a job did your super-
    visors or bosses think you were
    doing on that job — very good,
    fairly good, or not too good?

                                              Very good_____
                                              Fairly good_____
                                              Not too good_____

37. How good a job did you think
    you were doing?

                                              Very good_____
                                              Fairly good_____
                                              Not too good_____

38. Did your drug habit cause you
    to lose days of work on that job?

                                                      Yes_____
                                                       No_____

    IF YES:
    A) About how many days a month would
       you miss work because of your
       drug habit?   #_____

39. Did you ever injure yourself
    on that job?

                                                      Yes_____
                                                       No_____

    IF YES:
    A) Did that have anything to do
       with your drug use?

                                                      Yes_____
                                                       No_____

IF YES:
A) What?

---

40. Did you ever cause any damage
to equipment at work?

Yes_____
No_____

IF YES:
A) Did it have anything to do with
your drug use?

Yes_____
No_____

IF YES:
A) What?

---

41. Did you ever hurt anyone on this job?

Yes_____
No_____

IF YES:
A) Did it have anything to do with
your drug use?

Yes_____
No_____

IF YES:
A) What?

---

42. About how much was it costing you
    then on the average each day for
    the drugs you were using? $_____

43. How did you keep your habit from
    getting higher during this time?

    _____

44. How many people worked in your
    section at this company?

                                                   #_____

45. All told, about how many people
    worked at the place where you
    were working?

                                                   #_____

46. How many of the people in your
    section were addicts?

                                                   #_____

47. How many of the people who
    worked in your company were
    addicts?

                                                   #_____

48. How many people in your section
    were smoking marijuana on the job?

                                                   #_____

49. How many of all the people who
    worked in your company were
    smoking pot on the job?

                                                   #_____

50. Were you able to buy the drugs
    you used at the place where
    you worked?

                                                    Yes_____
                                                     No_____
                                            Only some_____

51. Did you sell drugs to any of the
    people who worked in your place?

                                                    Yes_____
                                                     No_____

52. Did your bosses know that you
    were using drugs?

                                                    Yes_____
                                                     No_____

    IF YES:
    A) What did they do about it?

_____

53. Apart from your bosses, did any of
    the people you worked with know
    that you were using drugs?

                                                    Yes_____
                                                     No_____

    IF YES:
    A) About how many of them knew?

                                                      #_____

B) What did they think about it:
did they approve, did they
disapprove, or didn't they
care one way or another?

Approve_____
Disapprove_____
Not care_____

54. Did you get together with any of
the people you worked with to
use drugs on the job?

Yes_____
No_____

55. Did you and your friends who used
drugs on the job try to get any other
workers to <u>start</u> using drugs?

Yes_____
No_____

IF YES:
A) About how many other people at
your company were you able to
get to start using drugs?

#_____

56. Did any drug addict friend ever help
you get a job at his place of work?

Yes_____
No_____

57. Did you ever help an addict friend
get a job at a place where you worked?

Yes_____
No_____

58. Did you start using any drug for
the first time on any job you had?

Yes_____
No_____

IF YES:
A) Which drugs?

_____

59. How did you support your drug
habit while you held the job we've
been talking about? (WRITE DOWN
FULL ANSWER AND ALSO CHECK
APPROPRIATE BOX.)

Earnings_____
Criminal acts_____
Other (What?)_____

DECK III

60. Did you take money from your
place of work?

Yes_____
No_____

IF YES:
A) How much did you take each
day or week? $___day ___wk.

61. Did you take goods from your
place of work?

Yes_____
No_____

IF YES:
A) How much were you able to get
   for the goods you took each
   day/week? $___day ___wk.

IF NOT ALREADY LEARNED IN Q. 59:

62. Did you hustle or take money
    outside of work during this time?

                                                    Yes_____
                                                    No_____

63. During the time you had that job,
    were most of your real close
    friends addicts?

                                                    Yes_____
                                                    No_____

    IF YES:
    A) Did these real close addict friends
       also have full-time jobs then?

                                                    Yes_____
                                                    No_____
                                                    Both_____

    IF NO TO QUESTION 63:
    A) Were any of your real close
       friends addicts?

                                                    Yes_____
                                                    No_____

    IF YES:
    Did they hold full-time jobs?

                                                    Yes_____
                                                    No_____
                                                    Both_____

64. Did you spend most of your nonworking hours during that time
hanging out with other addicts?

                                                    Yes_____
                                                    No_____

65. What were your reasons for
leaving the job we've been
talking about?   Still has job_____

_____

A) Were there any other reasons
for your leaving?

_____

66. Have you ever been arrested?

                                                    Yes_____
                                                    No_____

IF YES:
A) How many times were you
arrested?   #_____

B) Have you ever been convicted?

                                                    Yes _____
                                                    No _____

IF CONVICTED:
1. How much time have you
served altogether?   ___yrs. ___mos.

C) Did you take the job we've been
talking about in order to satisfy
a condition of probation or to
look good before a judge?

Yes _____
No _____

And now for some questions about
your background:

67. How old were you on your last
birthday?   _____

68. Are you single, married, divorced,
or what?

Single_____
Married (incl. C.L.)_____
Separated_____
Divorced_____
Widowed_____
Other (Specify)_____

69. How many children do you have?   #_____

70. What was the last year of school
that you completed?

Eighth grade or less_____
Some high school_____
High school graduate_____
Some college_____
College graduate or more_____

71. What were your parents' occupations?

_____

_____

72. In what religion were you raised?

                                    Protestant_____
                                      Catholic_____
                                        Jewish_____
                                        Muslim_____
                            Other (What?)_____
                                          None_____

73. What is your religion now?

                                    Protestant_____
                                      Catholic_____
                                        Jewish_____
                                        Muslim_____
                            Other (What?)_____
                                          None_____

INTERVIEWER'S REPORT

1. Respondent's sex:

                                          Male_____
                                        Female_____

2. Respondent's ethnicity:

                                          White_____
                                          Black_____
                                  Puerto Rican_____
                    Other Spanish-speaking_____
                                          Other_____

3. Name of treatment program

    _____

4. Length of interview

    _____

5. Cooperation of respondent:

Very_____

Fairly_____

Not too_____

6. Interviewer's name

_____

INDEX

ABOUT THE AUTHOR

David Caplovitz, who is currently Professor of Sociology, Graduate School and University Center of the City University of New York, was educated at the University of Connecticut and Columbia University, where he received his Ph.D. He has taught at Columbia University, the University of Chicago, and Hunter College. The author of numerous articles and books, including the classic The Poor Pay More, Professor Caplovitz has most recently published The Religious Drop-Outs: Apostasy among College Graduates (with Fred Sherrow) and Consumers in Trouble: A Study of Debtors in Default.